American History on the Screen

A Teacher's Resource Book on Film and Video

Wendy S. Wilson and Gerald H. Herman

J. Weston Walch, Publisher

Portland, Maine

User's Guide
to
Walch Reproducible Books

As part of our general effort to provide educational materials which are as practical and economical as possible, we have designated this publication a "reproducible book." The designation means that purchase of the book includes purchase of the right to limited reproduction of all pages on which this symbol appears:

Here is the basic Walch policy: We grant to individual purchasers of this book the right to make sufficient copies of reproducible pages for use by all students of a single teacher. This permission is limited to a single teacher, and does not apply to entire schools or school systems, so institutions purchasing the book should pass the permission on to a single teacher. Copying of the book or its parts for resale is prohibited.

Any questions regarding this policy or requests to purchase further reproduction rights should be addressed to:

Permissions Editor
J. Weston Walch, Publisher
321 Valley Street • P. O. Box 658
Portland, Maine 04104-0658

—*J. Weston Walch, Publisher*

Wide World Photos, Inc.

1   2   3   4   5   6   7   8   9   10

ISBN 0-8251-2000-4

Contents

Teacher Introduction

"It is like writing history with lightning!" Woodrow Wilson exclaimed in 1915, upon viewing D.W. Griffith's film *The Birth of a Nation*. Today, we are fairly blasé about films and television programs that have, or purport to have, themes based on historical subjects. Yet it is an accepted fact today that, for many people, these media are their only glimpse of history outside of a formal classroom. For our students, films and television provide a chief source of entertainment and, sadly, in many cases the students totally accept what they see on the screen as absolute fact.

With this in mind, it is our purpose to present some sample films you can tie to a U.S. history curriculum and to give you some ideas about using these films in the most productive way possible. We hope you can use these films in a broader context as a means of stimulating media awareness and critical viewing skills in your students, as a means of turning "media-passive" students into "media-active" students who see the viewing of a film not as a comfortable break from classroom work, but as a lesson in critical analysis and historical interpretation.

To do this, we must look at ways films can be used in a history classroom. Students are taught to analyze historical documents. A film can be analyzed and studied in much the same way. Several major questions could be asked of the film document: What is the content of the film? What information does it convey or portray? How is the information affected or determined by the necessity to entertain as well as instruct? What influences were at work during the production of the film (e.g., censorship, monetary constraints, attitudes of society, background of producers)? How was the film received when it was released?

Recently, film and television producers have gone to great lengths to convince educators of the accuracy of their productions. Packets of promotional materials containing posters, lesson plans, and bibliographies are often sent out by the production company or sponsor to lure students and teachers into watching the film or program. In light of this, it is essential to maintain a critical stance. This is not to say that films should not be shown and enjoyed, but we must employ a bit of caution in the process. We must teach our students that in print and film, there is no such thing as a completely objective and unbiased historical account.

The films chosen for this book are presentations of history rather than documentations of history. That is, they are reenactments of historical events rather than documentary records of events, such as a newsreel or actuality footage. These historical presentation films may present historical content in four ways:

1. **As a factual record:** It is possible to use film to dramatize what happened in the past. Some directors have been very concerned to portray historical events accu-

rately; Richard Attenborough's *A Bridge Too Far* (1977) is an example. Occasionally historians act as advisers or even participate in the production of such films. A good example of this is the role Daniel J. Walkowitz played in the making of the television drama *Molders of Troy* (1979), which re-creates the struggles of iron molders in upstate New York in the years 1859 to 1876.

2. **To convey atmosphere:** It is common for history teachers to use fiction to convey a sense of the past—life-styles, values, or beliefs. Filmmakers have spent much money, time, and energy to make historical presentations—whether fact-based, fictional, or docudramatic (combining elements of each)—look real. Costumes, sets, weapons, and props are often carefully reconstructed to lend legitimacy to the production. Makers of fictional films like *Ragtime* (1981) take great care in creating an accurate setting (in this case, New York in 1906) for fictional events. Films loosely based on real characters or events, such as Barry Levinson's *Avalon* (1990), Woody Allen's *Radio Days* (1987), or Neil Simon's *Brighton Beach Memoirs* (1986), re-create with scrupulous honesty the look and sounds of the time period in which they are set. Makers of historical epics, such as James Cruze's *The Covered Wagon* (1923) and John Ford's *The Iron Horse* (1924), which used participants and their descendants as extras, John Wayne's *The Alamo* (1960), which re-created the San Antonio de Behar Mission, whatever the liberties it took with its historical characters, and *Glory* (1989) take great pains to create an accurate historical context for their stories.

3. **Analogy:** Occasionally media producers might use a historical event to point out or explain contemporary motives or actions, particularly when the contemporary event is controversial. *Sergeant York*, an idealized and partly fictional biographical film about an American World War I hero, was made in 1941 to convey a preparedness message to a country torn between interventionists and isolationists as World War II raged all around it. Similarly, many of President Woodrow Wilson's shortcomings in his handling of the Great War's peacemaking were glossed over in the 1944 biographical film called *Wilson* to present an interpretation designed to support Franklin Roosevelt's vision of a postwar United Nations. Ralph Nelson's graphic reenactment of the Sand Creek Massacre, *Soldier Blue* (1970), is transposed to the halfway point in the Indian Wars period of American history to draw a continuum between the army's attitude toward and treatment of Native Americans in the nineteenth century and its actions at My Lai (1970) in the then-ongoing Vietnam War.

4. **As a lesson in historiography:** Because the dramatic form used in films required consistent and relatively simple motivational interpretations, students can often learn how the time period in which the film was made interpreted historical (and by implication contemporary) personalities or events. The narrow Freudianism that displayed the evils of society as the cause of deviant behavior during the early cold war period can also be seen in contemporary dramas like *White Heat* (1949) and in such historical dramas as Gore Vidal's *The Left-Handed Gun* (1958), about Billy the Kid.

Media resources have expanded dramatically in recent years, with new titles available every month. The films we have selected to key to U.S. history units are readily available in videocassette form as well as 16mm film and are currently popular with U.S. history teachers. We provide a list of other appropriate films for each unit that were not as easily obtainable at the date of this publication. Since this situation changes rapidly, we have included a bibliography of media sources that you can use to check the availability of films. If you use films in videocassette form, you have the benefit of being able to easily pause the tape, rewind, or even (depending on the VCR) freeze the image. It is often less expensive to purchase the film on videotape than to rent it, and you have the added advantage of having the film ready for use when you need it rather than depending on the vagaries of renting, which may result in a film on the French Revolution arriving from a video supplier in the middle of your unit on World War I.

Reproducible student material contained in this book includes "A Student Introduction to Historical Films" (page *xxvii*), a "Film Analysis Guide Sheet" (page *xxix*), and a glossary entitled "Common Film Terms to Aid in Film Analysis" (page *xxxi*). Most units also include reproducible student pages consisting of a guide to what to watch for in a film and a worksheet that includes a vocabulary list and questions based on the film. We suggest that you hand out both the "Film Analysis Guide Sheet" and the unit reproducible pages to students before they view the particular film. The vocabulary lists refer specifically to terms used in the film or in the introductory materials provided in the unit. The terms can be reviewed by you with the students before they watch the film or can be defined by the students as part of their written assignment or during class discussion. Likewise, it is up to you how to use the worksheet questions—as a written assignment, a springboard for class discussion, or both.

You will find that Unit 15 is different from the previous units in that it provides a case study on how a historical event—the OK Corral gunfight in this instance—has been redefined by filmmakers immersed in responding to, or wishing to profit from, popular attitudes or beliefs that existed when each of the films was made. This unit analyzes three of the many film versions of the gunfight. The first, *My Darling Clementine*, was made just after World War II as the victorious Allies, including the United States and Soviet Union, were justifying their own participation in the war in the light of rising cold war tensions. The second, *Gunfight at the OK Corral*, appeared at the midpoint of the Eisenhower administration when Americans were acting abroad as the globe's police force, ferreting out Communists even if that meant supporting corrupt dictators, while uncovering organized crime at home and enjoying the material rewards of "melting pot" conformity. The third, *Doc*, was produced at the height of the disillusionment and polarization resulting from the Vietnam War and manifested in the antiwar, counterculture, and minority empowerment movements. The unit is written primarily for your own enrichment and to suggest additional ways in which the use of films can illuminate the study of U.S. history and its interpretive shifts. But these examples might also be used productively with a more advanced American history class, especially since (given the limited class time available) the first two films are widely available on videocassettes and laser discs and can be watched by students outside of class. Reproducible student question sheets have been provided for use with each individual film in the unit as well as questions that ask students to compare the disparate views of the three films on these events.

We hope that you will find ways to use films as positive teaching tools or to provide an active viewing experience for your class. In our role as social studies teachers, we now need to add critical viewing skills (or visual literacy) to the list of important abilities our students need to develop for life in our media-conscious society.

Bibliography

Guides to Media Use

Fraser, George MacDonald. *The Hollywood History of the World* (Beechtree Books, 1988).

Furtaw, Julia C., ed. *The Video Source Book* (Gale Research Inc., 1993).

Lacey, Richard. *Seeing With Feeling: Film in the Classroom* (Saunders, 1972).

Maynard, Richard A. *The Celluloid Curriculum: How to Use Movies in the Classroom* (Hayden Books, 1971).

Moraco, James. *How to Read a Film*, rev. ed. (Oxford University Press, 1981).

O'Connor, John E. *Discussions on Teaching 2: Teaching History with Film and Television* (American Historical Association, 1987).

O'Connor, John E., ed. *Image as Artifact: Historical Analysis of Film and Television* (Krieger, 1989).

O'Connor, John E., comp. *Image as Artifact: Video Compilation* (American Historical Association, 1988).

O'Connor, John E., and Jackson, Martin, eds. *American History/ American Film: Interpreting the Hollywood Image* (Unger, 1980).

Rebhorn, Marlettte. *Screening America, Using Hollywood Films to Teach History* (Lang, 1989).

Rollins, Peter C., ed. *Hollywood as Historian: American Film in a Cultural Context* (University of Kentucky, 1983).

Television Licensing Center. *T.L.C.* (Films Incorporated 1981–present).

Thomas, Tony. *Hollywood and the American Image* (Arlington House, 1981).

Toplin, Robert Brent. *The Cinematic Historian: Hollywood Interprets America* (University of Illinois Press, 1984).

Finder's Aids

Dorsey, William. *The Black Video Guide: Library Edition* (Video Publications Ltd. and NICEM, 1986).

Educational Film/Video Locater, 3rd ed. (Bowker and the Consortium of University Film Centers, 1986), 2 vols.

Educator's Guide to Free Audio and Video Materials, annual ed. (Educator's Progress Service).

Hitchen, Howard B., ed. *America on Film and Tape: A Topical Catalog of Audio Visual Resources for the Study of United States History, Society, and Culture* (Greenwood, 1985).

Leff, Leonard J. *Film Plots* (Pierian Press, 1983).

Limbach, James L., ed. *Feature Films: A Directory of Feature Films on 16mm and Videotape Available for Rental, Sale, and Lease,* 8th ed. (Bowker, 1985).

Maltin, Leonard. *Leonard Maltin's TV, Movies and Video Guide* (Signet, 1988, reissued yearly).

Martin, Mick, and Porter, Marsha. *Video Movie Guide* (Ballantine, 1987, reissued yearly).

Media Log: A Guide to Film, Television, and Radio Programs Supported by the National Endowment for the Humanities (1979–present).

Pratt, Douglas. *The Laser Video Disc Companion* (New York Zoetrope, 1992).

Proud to Be...A Black Video Collection, One Kendall Square, Bldg. 600, Suite 125, Cambridge, MA 02139. Send $1.00 for the latest catalog of over 100 titles of black videos.

Reed, Maxine K., ed. *The Video Source Book,* 7th ed. (National Video Clearinghouse, 1985).

Scheuer, Steven H., ed. *Movies on TV and Videocassette* (Bantam, 1993, issued yearly).

Videohound's Golden Movie Retriever (Visible Ink Press, 1993, updated annually).

Weaver, Elizabeth, ed. *Film Programmer's Guide to 16mm Rental,* 3rd ed. (Reel Research, 1980).

Guides to American Film

Abrash, Barbara, and Egan, Catherine, eds., *Mediating History: The MAP [Media Alternatives Project] Guide to Independent Video by and About African American, Asian American, Latino, and Native American People* (New York University Press, 1992).

Bogle, Donald. *Blacks in American Films and Television, An Illustrated Encyclopedia* (Simon and Schuster/Fireside, 1989).

Hardy, Phil. *The Encyclopedia of Western Movies* (Woodburt Press/Dalton Books, 1984).

Langman, Larry, and Borg, Ed. *Encyclopedia of American War Films* (Garland, 1989).

Sayre, Nora. *Running Time: Films of the Cold War* (Dial Press, 1982).

Wetta, Frank J., and Curley, Stephen J. *Celluloid Wars, A Guide to Film and the American Experience of War* (Greenwood, 1992).

Video Sources

Ambrose Video Publishing, Inc. 1290 Avenue of the Americas, Suite 2245, New York, NY 10104. (800) 526-4663

American Historical Association.

Angelika Films.

Budget Films. 4590 Santa Monica Blvd., Los Angeles, CA 90029. (213) 660-0187

CBS Fox Video. 1330 Avenue of the Americas, 5th Floor, New York, NY 10019. (212) 373-4800

Churchill Films and Video. 662 North Robertson Blvd., Los Angeles, CA 90069. (213) 657-5110

Clarity Education Productions.

Corinth Films. 410 East 62nd Street, New York, NY 10021. (212) 421-4770

Coronet Video. Distributed by Simon & Schuster Communications, 108 Wilmot Road, Deerfield, IL 60015. (800) 621-4770

CRM/McGraw-Hill Films. 674 Via de la Valle, P.O. Box 641, Del Mar, CA 92014.

Discount Video Tapes. 3711B West Clark Avenue, P.O. Box 7122, Burbank, CA 91510. (818) 843-3366

Evergreen Video Society. 213 West 35th Street, New York, NY 10001-4024. (800) 225-7783

Facets Video. 1517 W. Fullerton Avenue, Chicago, IL 60614. (312) 281-9075

Festival Films. 2841 Irving Avenue So., Minneapolis, MN 55408. (612) 870-4744

Films for the Humanities. P.O. Box 2053, Princeton, NJ 08543. (800) 257-5126

Films, Inc. 5547 N. Ravenswood Avenue, Chicago, IL 60640-1199. (800) 223-6246

Fox Video. 2121 Avenue of the Stars, 25th Floor, Los Angeles, CA 90067. (800) 800-2FOX

Hollywood Home Theatre. 1540 N. Highland Avenue, Hollywood, CA 90028. (800) 621-0849

HBO Video. 1370 Avenue of the Americas, New York, NY 10019. (800) 648-7650

Image Entertainment. 9333 Oso Ave., Chatsworth, CA 91311. (818) 407-9100

IVE (International Video Entertainment). 15400 Sherman Way, Suite 500, Van Nuys, CA 91406. (800) 423-7455

Ivy Classics Video. 725 Providence Rd., Suite 204, Charlotte, NC 28207. (704) 333-3991

Janus Films. (see Films, Inc.)

Key Video. 1211 Avenue of the Americas, Second Floor, New York, NY 10036. (212) 819-3238

Kit Parker Films. c/o Central Park Media, 250 West 57th Street, New York, NY 10019. (800) 833-7456

Learning Corporation of America. Distributed by Simon & Schuster Communications, 108 Wilmot Road, Deerfield, IL 60015. (800) 621-2131

Live Home Video. 15400 Sherman Way, Suite 500, Van Nuys, CA 91410. (800) 908-0303

Lorimar Home Video. 15838 N. 62nd St., Suite 100, Scotsdale, AZ 85254. (800) 345-1441

MCA Home Video. 70 Universal City Plaza, Universal City, CA 91608. (818) 777-4300

McGraw-Hill Films. 1221 Avenue of the Americas, New York, NY 10020. (212) 997-6572

Media Home Entertainment. 5730 Buckingham Parkway, Culver City, CA 90230. (213) 216-7900

MGM–UA Home Video. 1000 Washington Blvd., Culver City, CA 90232. (213) 280-6000

Modern Sound Pictures. 1402 Howard Street, Omaha, NE 68102. (800) 523-0823

Movies Unlimited. 6736 Castor Avenue, Philadelphia, PA 19149. (800) 523-0823

Museum of Modern Art (MOMA). New York, NY.

National Audio Visual Center. 8700 Edgeworth Drive, Capitol Heights, MD 20743-3701. (301) 763-1896

Nelson Entertainment.

New Line Cinema. 575 Eighth Avenue, New York, NY 10018. (212) 674-7460

New Yorker Films. 16 West 61st Street, New York, NY 10023. (212) 247-6110

Orion Home Video. 9 West 57th Street, New York, NY 10019. (212) 980-1117

Paramount Home Video. 5555 Melrose Avenue, Hollywood, CA 90038. (213) 468-5000

Past America Inc.

PBS Video. 1320 Braddock Place, Alexandria, VA 22314-1698. (800) 424-7963

Prestige Film & Video. 18 East 48th Street, Suite 1601, New York, NY 10017. (212) 888-2662

Prism Entertainment. 1888 Century Park East, Suite 1000, Los Angeles, CA 90067. (213) 277-3270

RCA–Columbia Pictures Home Video. 3500 West Olive Avenue, Burbank, CA 91505. (800) 722-2748

Republic Pictures Home Video. 12636 Beatrice Street, Los Angeles, CA 90066-0930. (310) 306-4040

RKO Video. 1608 Broadway, New York, NY 10019. (800) 942-4144

Swank Motion Pictures. 201 South Jefferson Avenue, St. Louis, MO 63103. (800) 325-3344

Thorn-EMI Video. 1370 Avenue of the Americas, New York, NY 10019. (212) 977-8990

Touchstone Home Video. 500 South Buena Vista Street, Burbank, CA 91521. (818) 840-6056

Trans-World Entertainment. 6464 Sunset Blvd., Suite 1100, Hollywood, CA 90028. (800) 521-0107

Turner Home Entertainment. P.O. Box 105366, Atlanta, GA 30348-5366. (404) 827-3066

Twyman Films. (see Kit Parker Films)

United Home Video. 4111 South Darlington Street, Suite 600, Tulsa, OK 74135. (800) 331-4077

USA Home Video. 21800 Burbank Blvd., #300, P.O. Box 4062, Woodland Hills, CA 91365. (800) 423-5558

Vestron Video. P.O. Box 10382, Stamford, CT 06901. (203) 978-5568

Video Yesteryear. Box C, Sandy Hook, CT 06482. (800) 243-0987

Walt Disney Home Video. 500 South Buena Vista Street, Burbank, CA 91521. (818) 840-1111

Warner Home Video. 4000 Warner Blvd., Burbank, CA 91522. (800) 323-4767

Zenger Video. 10200 Jefferson Blvd., Room 96, P.O. Box 802, Culver City, CA 90232-0802. (800) 421-4246

Master Index of Feature Films

Asterisked films are featured in depth in a unit. Other films are synopsized on the indicated page.

The Colonial Experience

The American Revolution

The Expansion of the New Nation

The Civil War

The West

World War I

The Twenties

The Great Depression

World War II

The Cold War

The Civil Rights Movement

Life in the Fifties and Sixties

The Vietnam War

See complete filmography in Unit 13.

The End of the Twentieth Century

The OK Corral Gunfight—A Case Study

A Layperson's Note on Copyright and Fair Use

Copyright is a delicate balancing effort undertaken by the federal government on the one hand to encourage intellectual and artistic creativity by ensuring a fair return for the artist's efforts (as well as profit-engendered distribution systems) while, on the other, to provide an environment in which these ideas and achievements can spread widely to be judged in public review and analysis. Educators have long relied on the doctrine of "fair use" to permit copyrighted materials to be used in their classrooms without prior authorization. The Copyright Law of 1976 substantially circumscribed the concept of fair use, while the results of the author-user conference that accompanied the law's development suggested specific guidelines of brevity, spontaneity, and "cumulative effect"—that is, the extent to which the use interferes with the author's potential market—to help determine whether projected use of copyrighted material is permissible under the law. Both because this was a compromise between users and authors and because the law attempted to encompass the range of print and electronic media invented since the 1905 law, these guidelines were necessarily vague. The new nonprint media have been an area of particular contention between authors and users, partly because of their ephemeral nature and broadcastability, and partly because of the threat posed to producers and distributors by the explosion in the availability and ease of duplication technologies.

The law in this area is still developing, and definitive conclusions are not yet possible. When films, tapes, or discs are purchased or rented from legitimate educational distributors, specific use licenses accompany them. Beyond this, it is probably legal to use other commercial tapes legitimately acquired by purchase, rental, or lease in direct face-to-face instruction, though not to broadcast them over closed-circuit, instructional, or broadcast radio or television systems without a specific license to do so. It is probably illegal to deposit them in libraries for casual listening or viewing, to play them publicly to general (even student) or paying audiences, or to use "pirated" tapes for these purposes. Copies made without permission from other tapes, films, or other recordings are, except for limited preservation purposes, considered pirated copies, even if the recordings from which they were obtained are legitimate.

Under certain circumstances, "off-air" copies may also be legally employed in this same face-to-face instruction for a very limited time before they must be erased, though these should probably be recorded at the site of their proposed "time-shifted" use. ("Off-air" recording means the recording of a televised program, such as a PBS documentary. "Time-shifted" use is the showing of a recorded videotape at a time to suit an individual's need, such as conforming to a specific class meeting time.) To facilitate such use, many educational distributors are offering to license such recordings for educational purposes for a set time or for "the life of the tape" as an alternative to more expensive rentals or purchases. In addition, specialized off-air and commercial copy-licensing clearinghouses are now in existence or are being formed.

The legitimacy of excerpting unauthorized clips or cuts for summary presentation, review, or critical analysis remains an open question (those seen or heard on television or radio previews or review programs are provided by the distributors for this use), and many areas of nonprint media use remain murky or undefined. It is therefore important to consult some of the many guides available from professional organizations, clearinghouses, or copyright experts and to seek legal advice (often available to the district level or through the local superintendent's office) where the fact or situation of the proposed media use raises questions or poses special problems.

A Student Introduction to Historical Films

You have probably heard the expressions "Seeing is believing" and "A picture is worth a thousand words." It may seem to you that a very truthful and certainly enjoyable way to learn history is through pictures—moving pictures, or films. It is true that films do provide us with presentations of historical events such as the Vietnam War or the French Revolution. Historical themes have been popular as long as motion pictures have been produced. It is also true, however, that films provide us with *interpretations* of historical personalities and events. Just as you have learned to be critical of print documents, you must bring that same critical eye to nonprint or media documents. It is important to learn critical viewing skills to use when you see media productions in your social studies classes, on television at home, or in the movies.

In order to use films to their full advantage, you should ask several major questions when viewing a film:

1. What is the content of the film? What information does it convey?

2. How and/or why was the film produced? What forces were at work during its production that might have affected its final form? (For example: Censorship? Background of the producers? Budgetary limitations?)

3. How was the film received when it came out? Was it popular? Did it have any effect on the attitudes of the people who saw it?

Since films are produced first of all to entertain and, perhaps, secondly to instruct, it is important to remember that few film producers are willing to risk the box office draw of their film for historical accuracy. If a choice is to be made between entertainment and historical fact, it might well be that the truth suffers. If this is so, why use a film for learning at all? Why not use all print materials such as textbooks and readings?

First, print materials, like films, involve interpretation and careful analysis to determine historical fact. Films can also be a valuable way of going back through time to experience the atmosphere of a period in the past or to "see" historical characters long dead. Many film production companies try very hard to make the settings for their historical presentation as accurate as possible. They employ historians to act as consultants to advise in the construction of sets, costume design, weaponry, transportation, manners, and other details. Sometimes historians play an even more central role in these proceedings. A good example of this is the film *Denmark Vesey's Rebellion* (1981). Noted American historian Robert B. Toplin acted as the project director for the film and was assisted by a scholarly panel to ensure not only the accuracy of the visual details (the film was shot at various southern locations including historic Charleston), but also, and more importantly, the faithfulness of the historical interpretation of what historians understand actually happened. Toplin participated in

(continued)

A Student Introduction to Historical Films
(continued)

every stage of the production, ensuring that the film of this 1822 slave rebellion would avoid stereotyping its characters or reduce complex and controversial events to a conventional Hollywood plot line. The resulting film, starring Yaphet Kotto, Ned Beatty, and Cleavon Little, was broadcast on the Public Broadcasting System as part of the *A House Divided* series, and won numerous awards.

When you watch films in class, complete assignments, and have class discussions, try to keep in mind what the purpose of a film is—primarily entertainment. Also, try to see in what ways the films provide a greater lesson in historical interpretation and critical analysis. Above all, enjoy the unique experience of actively evaluating and analyzing a film document rather than being a passive receiver of its message.

Name _____ Date _____

Film Analysis Guide Sheet

1. Title of the film _____

2. Date of production _____

3. Studio _____

4. Director _____

5.   **Major character**   **Actor/Actress**

    _____   _____

    _____   _____

    _____   _____

    _____   _____

    _____   _____

    _____   _____

    _____   _____

6. Historical event portrayed by the film _____

_____

7. Approximate dates covered by the film _____

8. Are any historical consultants listed in the credits? If so, who? _____

_____

_____

9. Synopsis of the plot _____

_____

_____

_____

_____

_____

(continued)

         xxix   *American History on the Screen*

Name _____ Date _____

Film Analysis Guide Sheet *(continued)*

10. Does this film portray the historical event or time period accurately? If so, how? (Note costuming, sets, scenery, props, manners, etc.)

_____

_____

_____

_____

11. How does this film deviate from the historical facts, or, in other words, what inaccuracies can you find in this film?

_____

_____

_____

_____

12. What cinematic devices (fades, dissolves, flashback, montage, split scene, bridging shots, etc.) did the filmmaker use to convey a meaning or feeling in this film? Give examples.

_____

_____

_____

_____

13. Does this film contain any underlying messages, or is it a straight narrative of a specific historical event?

_____

_____

14. In your opinion, of what use is this film in explaining or illuminating a historical event, figure, or time period?

_____

_____

_____

Common Film Terms to Aid in Film Analysis

actuality footage: Film or video that is not set up and/or dramatized; e.g., newsreel film.

audio: The sound in a film or broadcast.

backlighting: Using the main source of light behind a subject to silhouette the figure.

black comedy: Comedy that deals with macabre topics such as murder or nuclear war. *Dr. Strangelove* is a good example.

bridging shot: Shot that covers a jump in place or time, such as newspaper headlines, falling leaves, hands of a clock, or an airplane taking off.

camera angle: Angle at which a camera is pointed at a subject. A high-angle shot from above a subject can make the subject look small. A low-angle shot can make a subject look large.

cinematography: The art and science of motion picture photography. *Videography* is a term used to describe video photography.

closeup: Any close shot, usually of a subject's face.

credits: The list, usually at the end of a film, of the crew and cast of a production.

cut: The instantaneous switch from one image or scene to another.

crosscutting: Cutting between two or more scenes to portray parallel action—events that are occurring simultaneously.

dissolve: To fade out one image while fading in another.

docudramas: Actual historical events that are reenacted, often in fictionalized versions—for example, *Roots, Holocaust.*

documentary: Film that is generally, but not always or completely, not fictional, usually containing actuality footage, interviews, and a narration. *Documentary* is an elastic term that may include reenactments, still pictures, sound effects, stock footage, graphics, and/or interpretive materials.

dolly shot: Taking a shot with a camera moving on wheels (called a dolly). Also called a follow or tracking shot.

editor: The person who cuts and splices together the film into its final form. Editors in video do this electronically with computerized equipment.

(continued)

Common Film Terms to Aid in Film Analysis
(continued)

establishing shot: A wide shot that establishes the location of a scene for the viewer.

fade-in/-out: In a fade-in, the screen gradually changes from black to the image. In a fade-out, the image dissolves to black.

flashback: A scene that is brought into the film from the past. Sometimes almost an entire film can be a flashback from the present to the past, as in *Little Big Man*.

focus: The clarity or sharpness of an image.

foley: A largely manual process for introducing any nonmusical or nonspoken sound effect or noise as part of the postproduction process.

freeze frame: Stopping of an individual frame to give the impression of a still image or photograph.

gaffer: The chief electrician in a production. The *best boy* is the gaffer's assistant.

genre: The type of a film, such as science fiction, Western, or horror film.

grip: The person in charge of props, sometimes called the key grip.

mise en scène: What actually takes place on the set—the actors, direction, type of cameras, etc.

montage: (1) the editing of film; (2) editing shots together in such a way as to produce a total meaning different from the parts actually shown.

narrative: The story of a film.

over-the-shoulder shot: Shot used in interviews or dialogue where the camera is placed behind and to the side of one of the speakers to show a portion of his or her head and shoulders as well as the other speaker.

pan: The horizontal movement of the camera lens from left to right or right to left.

point-of-view shot: Also called a subjective shot, a shot that shows the scene from the point of view of one of the subjects.

reverse angle: A shot taken from the opposite side of a subject, from that previously shown, often to show a second person in a dialogue.

Common Film Terms to Aid in Film Analysis
(continued)

scene: A coherent segment of the film, made up of a number of shots, that takes place in one location and at one time period and usually revolves around one particular action.

sequence: A section of film containing a group of scenes that constitutes a more or less complete thought, very often beginning and ending with a cut, dissolve, or fade.

shot: A single unedited piece of film or video that is taken by a camera.

split screen: Section of film with two or more distinct images on the screen that are not superimposed and do not overlap.

stock footage: Film or video shot for one purpose but used for another, usually used as background or establishing material.

tilt: The vertical movement of the camera lens up and down.

videography: See cinematography.

voice-over: Narration in which the narrator is not seen, used often in documentaries and TV commercials.

wipe: An effect where one image pushes or "wipes" another image off the screen. Wipes can have many shapes and are used more in TV than in film.

zoom: Changing the focal length using the special lens of the camera to go from wide angle to telephoto or vice versa.

1776
AP/Wide World Photos

Glory
TriStar Pictures

The Grapes of Wrath
c. 1940 Twentieth Century-Fox Film Corporation. All rights reserved.

Dr. Stangelove or: How I Learned to Stop Worrying and Love the Bomb
AP/Wide World Photos

The Killing Fields
AP/Wide World Photos

Good Morning Vietnam
AP/Wide World Photos

The Colonial Experience

Teacher's Guide

Three Sovereigns for Sarah, Nightowl Productions, 1986. Directed by Philip Leacock, color, 172 minutes. Distributed on videotape by Prism Entertainment.

Background of the Film

This three-episode video was originally presented on Public Television. It is based on extensive research into the period of the Salem witch trials, notably the book *Salem Possessed: The Social Origins of Witchcraft* by Paul Boyer and Stephen Nissenbaum. The outbreak of hysteria in Salem, Massachusetts, in 1692, which resulted in the execution of nineteen people as witches, has been the subject of many books, stories, and plays such as *The Crucible* by Arthur Miller. This film looks at this event as part of a series of social and political disputes that occurred in Salem.

As early as 1700, Robert Calef wrote an analysis of the witch trials in Salem Village (now Danvers, Massachusetts) pointing to the serious social divisions in the village itself and the opposition felt by many villagers against the more worldly and affluent port, Salem Town. The inland Salem Village was far more rural, and subordinate to the influences of Salem Town. In 1689 Salem Village chose a new minister, and this engendered a division within the village itself. The man ultimately selected was Reverend Samuel Parris, a failed merchant who had never held a position in a church. A dispute between pro-Parris and anti-Parris factions left deep scars in the village community. Parris's most outspoken supporter was Thomas Putnam. Very vocal in his opposition to Parris was Joseph Putnam, Thomas's stepbrother, who had inherited their father's wealth. The film uses this rivalry as a focal point, again based on the research by Boyer, Nissenbaum, and others.

The theory presented is that the "afflicted" children began their accusations as a game. The adults then used the girls' afflictions and accusations as a way to get back at their enemies, especially those who had opposed Parris. Thomas Putnam's wife, Ann, was particularly instrumental in the accusations. She sought to avenge herself over the loss of her husband's inheritance as well as losses in her own family. Ann Putnam's family had lost land and status to the family of the three sisters, Rebecca Nurse, Mary Easty, and Sarah Cloyce. The movie presents these village divisions through the narration of the surviving sister, Sarah Cloyce, as she strives to clear her sisters' names.

The film's dialogue is based on original transcripts of the trial and Sarah's diary. The costumes, buildings, locations, and props attempt to be faithful to the late 1600's in America. Many of the original locations were used in Salem, Danvers, and Ipswich, Massachusetts. The script also gives a good glimpse of the fundamental religious nature of life in Puritan Massachusetts.

Synopsis of the Plot

Since it was made to be a television series, this film is in three episodes. Episode One begins in Boston in 1703. A woman in ill health, Sarah Cloyce, has come with her nephew, Samuel Nurse, to testify before magistrates at a private hearing. Sarah wishes to clear her sisters' names from the charge of witchcraft. She tells the judges a story of conspiracy and family rivalry in Salem Village, which led to the accusations of witchcraft.

In a flashback, the story returns to June 1689, when Salem Village was picking a new minister for its meetinghouse. Thomas Putnam wants Reverend Samuel Parris. He is opposed by his stepbrother, Joseph Putnam, one of the wealthiest village landholders. In November of 1689 Parris does become minister and preaches his first sermon in which he equates his supporters with holiness. In February 1692 Parris's daughter Betty, his niece Abigail Williams, and Ann Putnam, Jr., begin to have fits after practicing crystal reading with Tituba, Parris's West Indian slave. When a doctor is sent for, he proclaims that the children are bewitched. The children are finally brought together in Thomas Putnam's house and they name Tituba and two other women as witches.

During her testimony in 1703 Sarah explains to the judges how these girls were influenced by their guardians. The names came from adults such as Ann Putnam, rather than from the children themselves.

Back again in 1692 Sarah is visiting her ailing sister, Rebecca Nurse. She is joined by her other sister, Mary Easty. Rebecca's son, Samuel, and Joseph Putnam arrive to tell Rebecca that she is to be arrested for witchcraft.

Episode Two begins in March 1692, with an examination held in the Salem Village meetinghouse. The girls and Ann Putnam accuse Rebecca of being a witch. When the girls have fits, Rebecca is sent to trial for witchcraft along with Sarah Good, another woman of Salem Village.

When Samuel Parris preaches an inflammatory sermon, Sarah stands up and leaves, slamming the door behind her. The children then have fits and name Sarah as their tormentor. Sarah is later arrested. She is stripped and the women look for devil's marks. She is then brought before the magistrate to be examined. The children once more have hysterical fits and name Sarah as a witch. Sarah is taken to prison to await trial.

As Joseph and Samuel ride to find help, they pass an elderly man, Giles Corey, being pressed to death for refusing to plead either guilty or innocent of being a wizard.

In prison Sarah meets Tituba, who has confessed to being a witch. Tituba shows Sarah the wounds she has from being beaten until she confessed. More and more of the accused are filling the prison. As the episode ends, Mary Easty is arrested for witchcraft.

Episode Three begins with Mary Easty being acquitted for lack of evidence. She is rearrested though and thrown into prison when another child names her. The evidence used is "spectral evidence"—that Mary's specter has been tormenting her, the most difficult charge for defendants to deny. Rebecca Nurse is found guilty and sentenced to death. She is brought before her minister, Nicholas Noyes, and excommunicated. On July 19, 1692, Sarah Good and Rebecca Nurse are hanged.

Mary Easty is next brought to trial and found guilty. As time goes on, surrounding towns borrow the afflicted girls to point out witches in their communities. Despite the power of the girls, Parris's influence erodes and he loses his salary. On September 22, many more accused witches are hanged, not just from Salem, but other towns as well. Mary Easty is executed.

Sarah is taken from prison in Salem to a private jail to relieve overcrowding. Her health deteriorates in the poor conditions of her confinement. Finally, Samuel and Peter Cloyce come to free Sarah; the governor has issued a general pardon to all those accused. Ministers above Parris reject spectral evidence as proof of witchcraft.

The program moves forward again to 1703. Sarah presents evidence of a conspiracy to the magistrates. The judges state that while years may pass before any final judgment will be made on the accused, she and her sisters are absolved from wrong. They give Sarah three gold sovereigns as a symbol, one for each of the three sisters wrongly accused of witchcraft. The story ends with Sarah telling what happened to the primary accusers after the witch trials. Mary and Rebecca's names were completely cleared in 1711, and in 1712 Rebecca's excommunication was overturned. Sarah Cloyce died three weeks after the hearings and was buried with the three gold sovereigns.

Ideas for Class Discussion

The American colonies saw one of the last major outbursts of witchcraft hysteria in the civilized world. A good focus for class discussion might be to discern why this was so. Was Europe so far ahead intellectually due to the Scientific Revolution. Did the upheaval caused by the rise of the new scientific view of the world encourage a search for scapegoats? Or was there something inherent in American Puritanism that could account for this? *The Crucible* by Arthur Miller would be an appropriate reading to accompany the viewing of this film. In writing his play Miller was protesting the witch trial-like hysteria of the McCarthy era. Perhaps the economic and political background of the events in Salem can account for the witchcraft trials as suggested by Boyer and Nissenbaum in their book, just as McCarthy's outbursts had a definite political agenda. Is the desire for human gain or the desire to find someone to blame for unsettling change the unifying force in both cases?

Books and Materials Relating to This Film and Topic

Boyer, Paul, and Nissenbaum, Stephen. *Salem Possessed: The Social Origins of Witchcraft* (Harvard University Press, 1974).

Karlson, Carol F. *The Devil in the Shape of a Woman: Witchcraft in Colonial New England* (W.W. Norton, 1987).

Weisman, Richard. *Witchcraft, Magic, and Religion in 17th Century Massachusetts* (University of Massachusetts Press, 1984).

Zeinart, Karen. *The Salem Witchcraft Trials* (Franklin Watts, 1989).

Other Media Resources for This Time Period

Roanoke (1986, 180 minutes, PBS Video) A three-part, made-for-television movie about the early contacts between English explorers and settlers and the Algonquian-speaking native population along the North American coast of what is now North Carolina. The story is told through the relationship between Roanoke's governor and artist John White and two native warriors, Wanchese and Manteo.

Plymouth Aventure (1952, 102 minutes, Films, Inc.) This film deals with the founding of the Massachusetts colony.

The Scarlet Letter (1972, 94 minutes, Facets Video) Based on Hawthorne's classic tale of adultery in seventeenth-century Salem, Massachusetts.

The Last of the Mohicans (1992, 114 minutes, Films, Inc., Fox Video) Retells James Fenimore Cooper's frontier story, replacing the racism of the original with a careful re-creation of European–Native American relations at the time of the French and Indian War. The film is rated R because the violence of that conflict is realistically portrayed.

Unit 1: The Colonial Experience

Three Sovereigns for Sarah, Nightowl Productions, 1986. Directed by Philip Leacock.

Major Character	Actor/Actress
Sarah Cloyce	Vanessa Redgrave
Samuel Nurse	Ronald Hunter
Reverend Samuel Parris	Will Lyman
Rebecca Nurse	Phyllis Thaxter
Mary Easty	Kim Hunter
Chief magistrate	Patrick McGoohan
Joseph Putnam	John Dukakis
Thomas Putnam	Daniel von Bargen
Ann Putnam, Sr.	Maryann Plunkett

What to Watch For

This made-for-TV movie deals with an episode in American history that is both fascinating and repelling to many—the Salem witch trials of 1692. The film not only captures accurately the events of the time using the manuscripts of the trials and Sarah Cloyce's diary for dialogue, but gives us a glimpse of historical detective work into the past to uncover why these witch-hunts may have started. The hysterical accusations of witchcraft, which in 1692 pitted neighbor against neighbor in Salem Village (now Danvers), Massachusetts, has been a subject of investigation and hypothesis for three hundred years. Two historians, Paul Boyer and Stephen Nissenbaum, believe that they have successfully explained the reason for the start of these witchcraft accusations and for such widespread acceptance of the claims that resulted in hundreds of people being accused of being witches.

Boyer and Nissenbaum's well-accepted theory is that there was a conspiracy in Salem Village in the 1690's that pitted its less well-to-do people against their neighbors in the nearby and affluent Salem Town. The supporters of the controversial minister of Salem Village, Reverend Samuel Parris, particularly Ann Putnam, had personal and family grievances over land and inheritance against many of the accused who did not support Parris. The main character, Sarah Cloyce, sets out this theory in order to exonerate her two older sisters, Rebecca Nurse and Mary Easty, who were hanged for practicing witchcraft.

Note the costumes, props, buildings, and settings. These are accurate re-creations of seventeenth-century New England. Note also the importance of religion in this Puritan community. An interesting comparison could be made between our court system today and justice as it was practiced in 1692.

Name _____ Date _____

Unit 1: The Colonial Experience

Three Sovereigns for Sarah

Vocabulary

Excommunication

Magistrate

Meetinghouse

Puritan

Restitution

Specter

Witchcraft

Questions Based on the Film

1. What had happened in England in 1688 that affected the colonies and caused them, in Sarah's words, to "feel adrift"?

   _____

   _____

2. What economic and cultural differences were there between Salem Village and

   Salem Town? _____

   _____

   _____

3. Why did Ann Putnam have grievances against Sarah's family?

   _____

   _____

4. According to Sarah, why is Rebecca accused of witchcraft?

   _____

   _____

(continued)

Unit 1: The Colonial Experience

Three Sovereigns for Sarah (continued)

5. What are the tests for sorcery that are used at Sarah's trial?

    _____

    _____

6. Why did Tituba confess to being a witch? _____

    _____

    _____

7. Why was the sentence of excommunication the worst punishment for Rebecca
   Nurse? _____

    _____

8. Why did the witch-hunts finally stop? _____

    _____

    _____

9. What evidence of a conspiracy does Sarah present to the magistrates at Boston in
   1703? _____

    _____

Unit 2

The American Revolution

Teacher's Guide

1776, Columbia Pictures Corporation, 1972. Directed by Peter H. Hunt, color, 148 minutes. Distributed on videocassette by RCA–Columbia Pictures Home Video.

Background of the Film

1776 is based upon the musical play of the same name that opened on Broadway in 1969. The play was written by Peter Stone, a well-known writer for stage, screen, and television, and Sherman Edwards, a composer, lyricist, and former teacher of American history. The play won awards from the New York Critics Circle and the Antoinette Perry Awards Committee.

1776 is a re-creation of the days from May through July 1776 when the Second Continental Congress wrestled with the idea of independence from England, culminating in the adoption of the Declaration of Independence. The movie is faithful to the play as it was written. Historically, the play is quite faithful to the events of the time with a few changes to make the drama more orderly and understandable.

The characters are presented virtually as they are recorded in historical documents—from John Adams, who was "obnoxious and disliked" (his own words), to Rhode Island's Stephen Hopkins, who often did indeed enjoy distilled spirits and wore his black wide-brimmed hat at all times in the Chamber. Events also are transcribed accurately: Ben Franklin's illegitimate son was the royal governor of New Jersey; the New York delegation did abstain on many votes, including the one on independence; George Washington's "gloomy" dispatches did arrive on an average of three a day; and John Dickinson of Pennsylvania did refuse to sign the Declaration, although he then left Congress to enlist in the Continental Army where he served valiantly.

The authors of the play freely admitted changing certain historical facts for the sake of the dramatic plot. Two major alterations that occurred were: first, historically, the vote for independence had already been taken on July 2, before the Declaration was finally debated and approved; second, the Declaration was not signed on July 4, 1776, when it was proclaimed, but was signed over a period of several months, because many of the signers were not present at the time of ratification. These changes were made, in the second instance, in the same way that the famous Pine-Savage engraving of the signing (with all present) alters the facts, to provide a dramatic climax to the entire event.

The authors also had to surmise what the debate on the Declaration might have been like, since no records were kept of the debate itself. Fortunately, in his autobiography, Jefferson provided two versions of the Declaration: one as he had originally written it, and one as it was finally approved. The play's authors then could use the additions and deletions as a reference for their dramatic portrayal. The tally board used to record votes did not exist in the Chamber, but was added to the play to clarify the action. In addition, the courier's description of the battle at the Lexington village green was a constructed event, used by the authors to interject the feelings of the common people who were so affected by the decisions of the Continental Congress.

A common film and stage device in dealing with historical events is a telescoping of time and characters to simplify events for audiences. This was done here. The number of members of the Second Continental Congress is cut down and, in the play's treatment of John Adams's relationship with Abigail, dozens of their letters are edited and combined to convey their relationship.

None of these changes diminishes the value of this capturing of a central event in American history, which the authors hope will fill a void in the education of most citizens. (See the excellent "Historical Note by the Authors" in Peter Stone and Sherman Edwards's *1776*, Penguin Books, 1969.)

Synopsis of the Plot

The time is May 1776 and the setting is Philadelphia, where the Second Continental Congress is meeting. The universally disliked John Adams of Massachusetts is despondent over the inactivity of the Congress. He berates them and charges them to vote for independence, but the Congress shouts, "Sit Down, John!"

Adams finds Benjamin Franklin having his portrait painted. Franklin tells Adams to give up his idea for independence unless he can get someone else, less disliked, to propose it. It is decided that Richard Henry Lee of Virginia should get the Virginia House of Burgesses to propose a resolution for independence. In the next scene, it is June 7 and a new delegation arrives. The delegation finds that the Congress isn't meeting on time and, when the members do wander in, they are at odds with one another. Lee arrives from Virginia with a resolution for independence, but the Pennsylvania delegation opposes any such action. The ensuing debate shows a split between the New England delegations and those of the other Colonies. To Adams's chagrin, it is decided that the vote for independence must be unanimous. Adams suggests a postponement of the vote until a Declaration of Independence can be written to explain the reasons for and aims of this radical action. Thomas Jefferson is appointed to write the Declaration although he wishes to return home to his bride and is reluctant to set to the task of writing.

When the Congress meets on June 22, it receives another depressing message from General Washington about the condition of the troops. After the Congress recesses, Washington's courier and the Chamber caretaker sit in the hall and the messenger describes how his best friends were killed at the Battle of Lexington—a reminder of the serious nature of the conflict with England.

In the next scene Jefferson's Declaration is finally read to the Congress, which then proceeds to add to and change it as the month of June draws to a close. A great argument occurs over the issue of slavery, condemned by Jefferson in the Declaration. Jefferson, a slave owner, states that he has resolved to free his slaves. In a song, Edward Rutledge of South Carolina sings of the "triangle trade of molasses to rum to slaves" as an example of the hypocrisy of New England in opposing slavery while getting rich on its profits. Then the entire Southern delegation walks out and independence seems an unachievable goal unless the antislavery clause is deleted.

It is now July 2 and Congress once more meets to vote on independence. Adams gives in on the clause against slavery in order to secure the unanimous vote. The resolution is adopted and the members, except for Dickinson of Pennsylvania, agree to sign it. On July 4 the signing is completed as the (Liberty) bell in the tower is rung to celebrate the news. As one by one the delegates sign, the scene fades to the actual document.

Ideas for Class Discussion

A good topic for class discussion might be the effect of regional differences on the history of the United States. If regional differences could cause so much consternation in 1776, how much greater might those regional differences prove fifty or one hundred years hence? It certainly would be appropriate to have a copy of the Declaration of Independence in the classroom or even a copy for each student to study before viewing the film.

Books and Materials Relating to This Film and Topic

Becker, Carl L. *The Declaration of Independence: A Study in the History of Political Ideas* (Alfred A. Knopf, 1956).

Bowen, Catherine Drinker. *John Adams and the American Revolution* (Little, Brown and Co., 1950).

Donovan, Frank. *Mr. Jefferson's Declaration* (Dodd, Mead and Co., 1968).

Stone, Peter and Edwards, Sherman. *1776, A Musical Play* (Penguin Books, 1969).

Other Media Resources for This Time Period

Johnny Tremaine (1957, 80 minutes, Films, Inc./Walt Disney Home Video) This film re-creates the Boston Tea Party, Paul Revere's ride, and the battles at Lexington and Concord.

Revolution (1985, 125 minutes, Warner Home Video) An expensively made movie, but a bomb at the box office, culminating in the Battle of Yorktown.

Drums Along the Mohawk (1939, 103 minutes, Films, Inc./Key Video) Directed by John Ford, this film takes place in the Mohawk Valley where Indian tribes loyal to the British posed a threat to settlers during the Revolution.

The Howards of Virginia (1940, 122 minutes. Budget Films/RCA–Columbia Pictures Home Video) Stars Cary Grant as a land surveyor who gets caught up in the Revolution.

America (1924, 95 minutes, Museum of Modern Art/Facets Video) D.W. Griffith's silent era epic of the war. Its battle scenes, tableaus of famous events, and period re-creations still hold up quite well, though a sappy love story mars the overall effect.

Unit 2: The American Revolution

1776, Columbia Pictures Corporation, 1972. Directed by Peter H. Hunt.

Major Character	Actor/Actress
John Adams	William Daniels
Benjamin Franklin	Howard Da Silva
Thomas Jefferson	Ken Howard
John Dickinson	Donald Madden
Edward Rutledge	John Cullum
Richard Henry Lee	Ron Holgate
John Hancock	David Ford
Abigail Adams	Virginia Vestoff
Martha Washington	Blythe Danner

What to Watch For

This film is based upon the award-winning musical play of the same name. It is a re-creation of the days from May to July 4, 1776, when the Second Continental Congress was meeting in Philadelphia. The Congress was attempting to deal with the idea of independence from England and its debate culminated in the adoption of the Declaration of Independence. Historically, the film is very faithful to the characters and events of the time. The authors made use of an extensive bibliography of original documents and books written about the period and the Congress's participants. John Adams was very much disliked, Thomas Jefferson was a fine violinist and was asked daily by Congress for a weather report, Benjamin Franklin often arrived in a sedan chair carried by convicts, and Caesar Rodney of Delaware was suffering from skin cancer.

In the debates of the Congress, notice the issues that were brought up and the regional disputes that developed, particularly between the New England states' representatives and the rest of the delegates. Boston and Massachusetts were often regarded as hotbeds of radical agitation and there was a continuing fear that one region would control the others. States rights versus federal rights was a common theme running through the proceedings.

Note particularly the debate over the antislavery clause in the Declaration that Jefferson had written. Jefferson was a slave owner, but had resolved to set his own slaves free. Edward Rutledge's song on the "triangle trade of molasses to rum to slaves" refers to the economic realities of the times and how slavery did not just benefit the South, but brought monetary wealth to New England as well. In an interesting aside, John Adams's cousin Sam Adams prophesied that "If we give in on this issue [slavery], there will be trouble a hundred years hence; posterity will never forgive us."(Quoted in Peter Stone and Sherman Edwards's *1776*, Penguin Books, 1969, p. 169.) The authors did not include these words in the play, because they felt that audiences would believe them to be invented. Often history does provide us with facts that seem more dramatic than fiction.

Unit 2: The American Revolution

1776

Vocabulary

Inalienable

Necessary

Continental Congress

Treason

Saltpeter

Triangle trade

Questions Based on the Film

1. How does the dress and demeanor of the delegates to the Continental Congress suggest regional diversity? _____

   _____

   _____

2. Why is Virginia chosen to propose the resolution for independence? _____

   _____

   _____

3. What are Pennsylvania representative John Dickinson's objections to the resolution for independence? _____

   _____

   _____

4. In his Declaration, why does Jefferson refer to the English king as a tyrant?

   _____

5. Why does Edward Rutledge of South Carolina object to the Declaration? How does he point out the hypocrisy of the North? How is the issue resolved?

   _____

   _____

Unit 3

The Expansion of the New Nation

Teacher's Guide

The Buccaneer, Paramount Pictures, 1958. Directed by Anthony Quinn, color, 121 minutes. Distributed on videocassette by Facets Multimedia.

Background of the Film

This time period in American history (the first two decades of the nineteenth century) is a difficult one to explore with feature films. The problem is that filmmakers seem to be infatuated with the romance and legend of this time frame and often sacrifice historical accuracy in order to tell a good story. Thus figures like Daniel Boone, Dolly Madison, Davy Crockett, and Andrew Jackson evolve into folk heroes and it becomes difficult to separate myth from fact. The movie *The Buccaneer* is typical of this genre in its dealings with Jean Lafitte (also spelled Laffite), the French-born pirate and adventurer who helped Andrew Jackson at the Battle of New Orleans in 1815.

Lafitte's life story is certainly one that lends itself to drama. Jean and his brother Pierre owned a blacksmith shop in New Orleans as early as 1809. They also operated a smuggling ring out of a base on Barataria Bay, south of New Orleans, in the period following the U.S. acquisition from France of the Louisiana Territory. Lafitte's "privateers," as he called them, claimed to attack ships belonging to Spain and sailed under the Bolivian flag with "letters of marque." This written authority from the government gave them the right to prey upon Spanish vessels as privateers, rather than as outright pirates. It is believed that they attacked ships of many nations, although by declaring American ships off limits, Lafitte was careful to avoid antagonizing the citizens of New Orleans. Public opinion generally accepted the privateers. Many citizens purchased the goods smuggled in by them, much to the dismay of U.S. Customs officials.

Louisiana Governor William C. Claiborne was opposed to Lafitte's illegal activities, but after the outbreak of the War of 1812, he became more concerned over the prospect of a British invasion. In 1814 a British commander offered Lafitte $30,000 and a commission in the British Navy if he would cooperate with the British in an attack upon New Orleans. Lafitte went to Governor Claiborne with the British plan and offered his services to defend the city in return for a pardon. Claiborne turned down Lafitte's offer and the base at Barataria was attacked and destroyed by U.S. forces. Lafitte then presented his offer to General Andrew Jackson, who had arrived with troops to defend New Orleans. Badly undermanned and lacking armaments, Jackson accepted Lafitte's offer and granted the pirates a full pardon, in return for their help in fighting the British. The pirates fought alongside Jackson's forces and, because of their gunnery experience, greatly aided in securing an American victory at the Battle of New Orleans, which was actually fought after the War of 1812 had ended.

After the battle Lafitte became the toast of New Orleans; he attended the victory ball and became friendly with Governor Claiborne. Public opinion veered against Lafitte once the British threat was ended and stories emerged of jewelry belonging to a Creole lady being found among the loot at Barataria, taken as proof that Lafitte's men did rob American ships. In 1817 Lafitte and his men sailed to Galveston Island off the coast of Texas—then a part of Mexico—and built a new base called Campeche. From Campeche, Lafitte's men prospered by preying on Spanish ships. Whether by Lafitte's command or not, many of his men engaged in open piracy on all ships. The U.S. government sent a warship to demand that Lafitte abandon Galveston. In 1821 Lafitte burned Campeche and sailed off to parts unknown.

The movie embellishes this story by adding a love interest for Lafitte, the governor's daughter Annette—a totally fictitious liaison. A subplot is woven in involving one of Lafitte's captains, Brown, who is hanged by Lafitte for capturing an American ship and killing Annette's sister, who is on board. Lafitte did hang Brown for disobeying orders, but this event occurred years later, in 1819, after Brown and his men had looted a plantation, not a ship. In the film, at the Battle of New Orleans on January 8, 1815, Lafitte and his men arrive at the last minute to save the day. In reality, the Baratarians had been fighting with Jackson's forces for several weeks. Dominique You, Lafitte's closest comrade, did prove himself an able artilleryman and was commended by Jackson for his valor and skill.

This movie was a remake of the 1938 version, also called *The Buccaneer*, and was directed by Cecil B. deMille. Anthony Quinn (deMille's son-in-law) played a minor role in the 1938 movie and went on to direct this 1958 movie. This was the last movie produced by Cecil B. deMille.

Synopsis of the Plot

The movie opens in the camp of General Andrew Jackson. The British have captured Washington and burned the capitol. Jackson has only 1,200 poorly trained and equipped men to oppose the British, who have landed on the Louisiana gulf coast and are advancing on New Orleans with an invasion force of 16,000.

The scene switches to the market of Jean Lafitte, where the citizens of New Orleans are buying smuggled goods. Governor Claiborne arrives to declare that he will give $500 for Lafitte, dead or alive.

On a New Orleans wharf, a ship is departing with a large gold shipment. In Barataria, the pirates are coming back empty-handed; the captains want to sink American ships. Lafitte sets sail to prevent a renegade captain named Brown from raiding an American ship. Brown has captured the *Corinthian*, killed the crew and passengers, and stolen the gold. Lafitte boards Brown's ship and hangs him for disobeying orders.

British warships sail into Barataria and the British commanders meet with Lafitte. They offer him $30,000 in gold and a commission in the British Navy if he will join them in fighting the Americans. Instead, Lafitte goes to Governor Claiborne with the British documents and offers to help the Americans in return for a pardon for himself and his men. The governor's council is opposed to this, and when Lafitte returns to Barataria, he finds that the Americans have destroyed his base and that his men have been thrown in prison.

Jackson arrives in New Orleans and receives word that the British fleet is within thirty miles of New Orleans. Lafitte enters Jackson's quarters and tries to convince the general to grant his men a pardon in return for badly needed gunflints and powder. A planter arrives to say that the British are eight miles from New Orleans. Jackson and Lafitte make a deal.

Lafitte goes to the prison and frees Dominique You, telling him that the men will get a pardon if they fight for Jackson. In the bayou Jackson and his men are preparing to meet the British. Lafitte and his men come out of the swamp with ammunition. Thanks to the aid of the pirates, Jackson is victorious.

A victory dance is held and Lafitte is the center of attention until the cabin boy, the sole survivor of the ship *Corinthian*, is questioned by a crowd. Lafitte admits that his men were responsible for the sinking of the ship. Although Jackson steps in to prevent Lafitte's lynching by the crowd, Lafitte claims that all he wishes is a one-hour head start. The film ends with Lafitte and his companions sailing out into the open sea.

Ideas for Class Discussion

This unit lends itself to a study and/or discussion of American heroes. Why do we seem to need larger-than-life personalities in this time period? Is it a young nation's need for legitimacy, tradition, or myth? Ask students to read folk myths and tales such as the Jim Bowie, Davy Crockett, John Henry, or Johnny Appleseed stories, which emerged from the same period. Why do Andrew Jackson and Davy Crockett end up as folk heroes, and not Jean Lafitte?

Books and Materials Relating to This Film and Topic

Saxon, Lyle. *Lafitte the Pirate* (The Century Co., 1930; reprinted 1989, Pelican). The historical novel on which the film is based.

Fraser, George MacDonald. *The Hollywood History of the World* (Beechtree Books, 1988).

Gonzales, Catherine Troxell. *Lafitte: the Terror of the Gulf—Stories for Young Americans* series (Panda Books, 1981).

Hickey, Donald R. *War of Eighteen-twelve, A Forgotten Conflict* (University of Illinois Press, 1989).

Myers, John M. *Alamo* (1973, Bison).

Other Media Resources for This Time Period

The Alamo (1960, 199 minutes, Films, Inc./CBS–Fox Video) John Wayne's epic, if somewhat tendentious, re-creation of the holding action that gave Texas the time to organize its defense.

Davy Crockett: King of the Wild Frontier (1955, 93 minutes, Films, Inc./Walt Disney Home Video) Exemplifies the larger-than-life hero popular in this period of American history.

Unit 3: The Expansion of the New Nation

The Buccaneer, Paramount Pictures, 1958. Directed by Anthony Quinn. Based on the novel *Lafitte the Pirate* by Lyle Saxon.

Major Character	**Actor/Actress**
Jean Lafitte	Yul Brynner
Andrew Jackson	Charlton Heston
Dominique You	Charles Boyer
Governor Claiborne	E.G. Marshall
Annette Claiborne	Inger Stevens
Bonnie Brown	Claire Bloom
Ezra Peavey	Henry Hull
Mercier	Lorne Greene

What to Watch For

This film takes place in New Orleans during the time of the War of 1812. Jean Lafitte was a French-born smuggler/pirate who operated out of a base south of New Orleans called Barataria, despite efforts of U.S. government officials to stop him. General Andrew Jackson is sent to Louisiana to defend the area against attack by the British. Jackson's army is a ragged force of regular U.S. militiamen, volunteers from Kentucky and Tennessee, and Choctaw Indians. Jackson is forced to make a deal with Lafitte to gain ammunition and men for the defense of New Orleans. The film basically tells the story of Lafitte's "patriotism" for his adopted country and how Lafitte's aid made it possible to defeat the British at the Battle of New Orleans in 1815.

Unfortunately, the film romanticizes the story greatly and embellishes it with a fictional subplot about Lafitte's love for the daughter of Louisiana Governor Claiborne. Lafitte is shown to come to Jackson's aid at the last minute when in reality, Lafitte's men had been working with Jackson for several weeks. The episode concerning the renegade Captain Brown is also distorted. Lafitte did hang a Captain Brown for disobeying orders, but the event took place several years after the Battle of New Orleans, after Brown and his men had looted a plantation, not a ship.

Note the methods of fighting during the Battle of New Orleans. The rockets fired by the British, known as Congreve rockets (after their inventor), produced a "red glare" that Francis Scott Key wrote about in "The Star-Spangled Banner." Lafitte's men were skilled at artillery, which did help win the day.

This period of time in American history is often portrayed in films through the lives of larger-than-life heroes. Films like *The Buccaneer*, *Davy Crockett*, *The Iron Mistress* (about Jim Bowie), and *The Alamo* are very typical of films that glorified the early life of our nation.

Name _____ Date _____

Unit 3: The Expansion of the New Nation

The Buccaneer

Vocabulary

Bayou

Musket flints

Blockade

Privateer

Questions Based on the Film

1. What is the difference between a pirate and a privateer?

   _____

   _____

2. What was the strategic importance of New Orleans? _____

   _____

   _____

3. What is the deal that Lafitte makes with General Andrew Jackson as they learn
   that the British are advancing on New Orleans? _____

   _____

   _____

4. Describe the characters of Lafitte and Jackson as they are portrayed in the film.

   _____

   _____

   _____

5. Compare the British Army and its method of fighting with the army of Andrew
   Jackson. _____

   _____

6. Why is Lafitte forced to leave his adopted homeland? _____

   _____

   _____

Unit 4

The Civil War

Teacher's Guide

Glory, Tri-Star Pictures, 1989. Directed by Edward Zwick, color, 122 minutes. Distributed on videocassette by RCA–Columbia Pictures Home Video and available from Zenger Video with accompanying book. Received Academy Awards for Best Supporting Actor (Denzel Washington), Best Cinematography, and Best Sound.

Note: Although this film is rated R for violence, it is featured in school catalogs. You may wish to use a parental permission form.

Background of the Film

Glory has been hailed as one of the most historically accurate and realistic movies about the American Civil War. It is also a film that presents an aspect of history which is unknown to most Americans—the fact that by the end of the Civil War, African American soldiers made up twelve percent of the Union Army. There were 166 African American regiments in the Union Army and over 180,000 African American soldiers, many of whom had been slaves until within a few months of their enlistment.

Glory focuses on the formation of the Massachusetts 54th Regiment, its training, its efforts to be used in combat rather than as a labor force, and finally the 54th's heroic attack on Fort Wagner, South Carolina. The assault on Fort Wagner by the 600 men of the 54th was a turning point for the United States' recruitment of African American soldiers and, in many respects, a turning point in the fight for the abolition of slavery. As one abolitionist commented: "Who asks now in doubt and derision, 'Will the Negro fight?' The answer is spoken from the cannon's mouth…it comes to us from…those graves beneath Fort Wagner's walls, which the American people will surely never forget." (James M. McPherson, "The 'Glory' Story." *The New Republic*, January 8 and 15, 1990, p. 23.)

Robert Gould Shaw was the son of prominent Boston abolitionists. He quit Harvard in his junior year to join the Union Army. He was wounded at Antietam Creek in

1862 and became disillusioned by the savagery of the bloodshed. When Massachusetts Governor John Albion Andrew, encouraged by the black leader Frederick Douglass, commissioned an all-African American regiment, 23-year-old Shaw was offered the command. Douglass's two sons enlisted in the 54th and Lewis Douglass was sergeant-major of the regiment from its beginning, a fact not brought out by the film.

Shaw is the only principal character in the film who is not fictitious. Some historians have wondered why real historical characters were not used, such as Garth Wilkinson James, brother of William and Henry James, who was the adjutant of the regiment, the Douglass brothers, or Sergeant William H. Carney, the first African American to win the Congressional Medal of Honor for heroism. Moreover, where the movie gives the impression that most of the soldiers of the 54th were former slaves, the regiment was predominantly made up of African Americans from the North who had always been free. It is true that most of the 180,000 African American soldiers who eventually served in the Union Army were former slaves, and *Glory* can be understood as an attempt to universalize the 54th's experience.

Despite a few inaccuracies, such as the 54th attacking the fort from the north instead of from the south, attention was paid to the historical detail of the events themselves. Civil War historian/novelist Shelby Foote acted as a consultant on the film. The African American soldiers, with Shaw's support, did refuse to accept unequal pay (Congress approved equal pay in 1864). The shoes actually delivered to the men had no left or right; you simply wore them until they became left and right. The close order of the battle lines shown with the massing of men shoulder to shoulder is what accounted for the high casualties during the Civil War. Civil War "reenactors" were used, including thirty-eight African American reenactors. Reenactors are Civil War buffs who have authentic uniforms and weapons and participate in re-creations or reenactments of Civil War battles. Colonel Shaw did dismount his horse and lead his men in attacking the fort. His body was thrown into a common grave with his men. When a Union commander requested the return of Shaw's body, a Confederate officer replied, "We have buried him with his niggers." Later, when a Union officer tried to recover the body, Shaw's father wrote to stop him, saying that this was the most appropriate burial place, the field where he had fallen.

There is a monument in Boston to Shaw and the 54th Regiment sculpted in bas-relief by Augustus St. Gaudens, showing the colonel on his horse surrounded by his proudly marching men. The closing credits of the movie are run over shots of this monument.

Aside from the fictionalized (and some charge, stereotypical) characters and the overemphasis on escaped slaves within the ranks of the 54th, critics of the film have questioned the centering of the story on Shaw and his white subordinates, rather than on the African Americans who, in order to fight for freedom, struggled against Northern prejudice and Southern threats that they would not be treated as war prisoners if captured bearing arms against the Confederacy. Finally, since the film ends in the bloody and unsuccessful Fort Wagner battle, the film inevitably raises the question of the meaning of the term "glory" itself, juxtaposing all the heroic paraphernalia of traditional war films' climaxes against the futility and slaughter of the event itself. Interestingly, movie critics mostly questioned the casting of the obviously youthful and uncommanding Matthew Broderick as Colonel Shaw, because it ran counter to the conventions of heroic commanders in the expectations of Hollywood.

Synopsis of the Plot

The movie opens at Antietam Creek, Maryland, in 1862. Twenty-three-year-old Robert Gould Shaw is wounded during the Confederate rout of Union forces. In a field hospital, Shaw hears that Lincoln is going to free the slaves.

At home in Boston, Shaw meets Frederick Douglass and Governor Andrew at a reception. The governor proposes to raise a regiment of Negro soldiers and Shaw's name has been submitted as commander. Shaw's friend, Cabot Forbes, chides him for accepting, but ends up joining him.

Shaw surveys his prospective troops who include his well-educated friend Thomas Searles as well as illiterate field hands. They are marched to a camp at Readville, Massachusetts, just outside of Boston, past white soldiers making derisive comments. To train and bring discipline to the unit, Shaw brings in a tough Irish drill sergeant named Mulcahy.

The government finally sends guns to the regiment and Shaw drills them in the proper use of the weapons. Forbes confronts Shaw about why he is treating the men so harshly.

Shaw goes to the officers' mess for Christmas, where his fellow officers are condescending to him because of his command of the 54th. Meanwhile, Trip, one of Shaw's men, has deserted to find some shoes. He is captured and Shaw orders him publicly flogged. Rawlins informs Shaw that shoes are a necessity and Shaw goes to the quartermaster to get shoes, by force if necessary, for his men. He is successful.

When payday arrives, Shaw reads a letter from the government that the regiment will be paid $10 per month, $3 less than white soldiers. The soldiers refuse to accept any pay and Shaw rips up his pay as well. The long-awaited uniforms arrive and the 54th marches down the main street of Boston to its first assignment.

The 54th is sent south and Rawlins is made a sergeant major. The men arrive in Beaufort, South Carolina, on June 9, 1863. There is very little action there and it becomes clear that they are only to be used as a labor force. Shaw finally confronts the commanding officer at Beaufort with the knowledge of irregularities and forces him to transfer his men to a combat unit. At James Island, they meet and repel a Confederate force.

The Union commanders decide to try to take Fort Wagner, a coastal installation that protects Charleston, South Carolina. Shaw volunteers the 54th to lead the attack, an almost suicidal task due to the lack of cover along the open sandy beach that must be crossed and the ocean limiting maneuvering room. The men sing spirituals that night and prepare themselves for battle.

As Shaw's men march by the white soldiers, they are cheered. Shaw sends his horse back to the Union lines and joins his men on foot. They charge Fort Wagner, get to the dunes, then wait until dark when they mount the attack on the fort's sand parapets under fierce bombardment. Shaw is killed going up the embankment, but his troops fight on. The next day, the dead of the 54th cover the beach. They have failed to take the fort. The Confederates bury Shaw with his men in a mass grave. Closing graphics state that the fort was never taken, but that the conduct of the 54th Regiment was an important breakthrough in the acceptance of black troops in the war.

Ideas for Class Discussion

The film's title itself can serve as a discussion topic, especially in light of the reemergence of the virtues of military prowess in the wake of the "techno-war" in the Persian Gulf. Why was the film titled *Glory?* In what sense is what happened to these men glorious? Is the term used positively or cynically? Other topics might include the questions raised by critics about the liberties taken by the filmmakers with the re-creation of the battle for Fort Wagner itself, the focus of the film on the regiment's Caucasian officers, and the substitution of stereotypical characters for portrayals of the real African Americans who went to war for the Union in the Civil War.

Books and Materials Relating to This Film and Topic

Benson, Richard, with commentary by Lincoln Kirstein. *Lay This Laurel* (Eakins Press Foundation, 1973).

Burchard, Peter. *Glory* (St. Martin, 1989).

Burchard, Peter. *One Gallant Rush* (St. Martin, 1989).

McPherson, James M. *Battle Cry of Freedom: The Civil War Era* (Oxford University Press, 1988).

McPherson, James M. "The *Glory* Story" (*The New Republic*, January 8 and 15, 1990, pp. 22–28).

Pyron, Darolen Asbury, ed. *Recasting: "Gone with the Wind" in American Culture* (University Presses of Florida, 1983).

Other Media Resources for This Time Period

Abe Lincoln of Illinois (1940, 110 minutes, Films, Inc./Coronet Video) The film version of Robert E. Sherwood's reverential play with Raymond Massey reprising his Broadway triumph as the young Illinois lawyer matured by the loss of his great love. It is mostly faithful to the history on which it is based.

Across Five Aprils (1986, 29 minutes, Random House Video/Zenger Video) Dramatizes the effects of the Civil War on the home front. Based on the story by Irene Hunt.

The Andersonville Trial (1970, 150 minutes, Zenger Video/Coronet Video) An excellent PBS Hollywood Television Theater version of the 1865 war-crimes trial of a Confederate captain held responsible for the deaths from starvation or disease of some 15,000 Union prisoners of war. It was based on MacKinley Kantor's novel.

Denmark Vesey's Rebellion (1981, 90 minutes) About an abortive slave revolt in South Carolina in 1822; *Solomon Northrup's Odyssey* (1984, 120 minutes) about a free African American kidnapped into slavery in Louisiana until rescued in 1853; and *Experiment in Freedom: Charlotte Foster's Mission* (1985, 125 minutes) about a wealthy Philadelphia woman who risks everything to start a community of freed slaves on the South Carolina sea islands during the Civil War are three parts of the PBS *A House Divided* series on which historian Robert Toplin worked. They are available individually on video from Past America Inc.

The General (1927, 74 minutes, Swank Motion Pictures/HBO Video) Buster Keaton's silent classic about the unsuccessful 1862 exploit by Union spies led by James J. Andrews, who stole a Confederate train near Atlanta, planning to run it to Chattanooga, destroying bridges, supply depots, and telegraph lines as they went. They were pursued and most were captured and hanged (a fate omitted from the film) by Confederates in other trains. A more serious sound version of the story, called *The Great Locomotive Chase* (1956, 85 minutes, Films, Inc./Walt Disney Home Video) also exists.

Gone with the Wind (1939, 219 minutes, Films, Inc./MGM–UA Home Video) David O. Selznick's film of Margaret Mitchell's novel spectacularly re-creates Sherman's destruction of Atlanta. But, in order to walk a fine line between depression and preparedness values and between northern liberal and southern conservative opinion, Selznick presented a sanitized, nostalgic and, in some ways, simple-minded antebellum South in contrast to the complex ambivalence about the South, its family traditions, and its "peculiar institution" of the Mitchell novel. The film's script and production values reflect a moment in the history of American and Hollywood consciousness and of the Southern renaissance of the 1930's as much (or more) than they do the history of the Civil War. Precisely because this film (especially since its recent restored theatrical rerelease) is so much a part of many people's subconscious vision of the Civil War, if it is shown, it should be screened with great care.

The Horse Soldiers (1959, 119 minutes, Films, Inc./MGM–UA Home Video) John Ford's recasting of Union Colonel Benjamin H. Grierson's 1,700-man raid 300 miles inside Mississippi to cut Confederate supply lines to Vicksburg. Unlike John Wayne's rough-hewn portrayal of Colonel Marlow, a railroad engineer, Grierson was actually an Illinois music teacher before the war. But scenes like the Union destruction of Newton Station and the attack by Confederate military-school students on the Union force are reflections of fact, though, unlike the film, the Northern forces actually cut them down.

The Red Badge of Courage (1951, 70 minutes, Films, Inc./Facets Video/Zenger Video) Directed by John Huston and starring Audie Murphy, this version of Stephen Crane's novel portrays the experiences of a young soldier in the Civil War.

The True Story of Glory Continues (1991, 45 minutes, RCA–Columbia Pictures Home Video) The background and continuation video produced as a companion piece to the film *Glory*.

Unit 4: The Civil War

Glory, Tri-Star Pictures, 1989. Directed by Edward Zwick.

Major Character	**Actor/Actress**
Colonel Robert Gould Shaw	Matthew Broderick
John Rawlins	Morgan Freeman
Trip	Denzel Washington
Cabot Forbes	Cary Elwes
Thomas Searles	André Braugher
Shirts	Jihmi Kennedy
Sergeant Mulcahy	John Finn

What to Watch For

Glory brings to light the little-known story of the formation of one of the first all-African American regiments during the Civil War and its heroic assault on Fort Wagner, South Carolina. The 54th Massachusetts Regiment was formed in Boston at the urging of Abolitionists and the prominent African American leader, Frederick Douglass, who is briefly portrayed in the film. Douglass felt it was important that Negroes take part in a war that, especially after the Emancipation Proclamation, was being fought to gain their freedom. It was also hoped that African American regiments would dispel the stereotype of African Americans as lazy, shiftless, and cowardly. Watch for examples of this stereotyping in the film. The gallant assault on Fort Wagner proved the courage and discipline of the African American regiments and by the end of the war, African American soldiers made up twelve percent of the total Union forces.

Despite the impression given by the movie, most of the 54th Regiment were Northern African Americans who had been free all their lives. Some Northern African Americans were well educated, like the character Thomas Searles. It is true, however, that most of the soldiers in the 166 African American regiments who fought in the Civil War had been slaves up until a few months before their enlistment.

This film does present an accurate picture of the Civil War era, particularly the method of fighting. Note how close the battle lines are with a massing of the soldiers shoulder to shoulder. This is what accounts for the terrible casualty rate of the Civil War, one of the highest in history. The willing sacrifice of the 54th at Fort Wagner created new levels of respect for the abilities and courage of African American soldiers throughout the Union Army, but the 54th's "glory" also raises disturbing questions about the nature of war itself, about the Fort Wagner tactics, and about the pointlessness of such sacrifices as a means of gaining respect. Fort Wagner remained

(continued)

Unit 4: The Civil War *(continued)*

in Confederate hands until the end of the war, and after the brief Reconstruction period, African American soldiers were reduced to menial tasks and garrison duty except on the American frontier where they performed heroically in the Indian wars.

The uniforms and weapons are replicas of those used. Notice that the shoes received by the 54th are all alike; there is no left or right. You wore the shoes until they stretched to become left and right.

Glory has stimulated interest in the role played by the black regiments in the Civil War, a previously forgotten chapter in African American history. "Reenactors," Civil War buffs who re-create the battles and camp life of the 1860's, now include more African American members among their ranks than before the release of this film.

Unit 4: The Civil War

Glory

Vocabulary

Abolitionist

Bayonet

Confederate

Contraband

Emancipation Proclamation

Union

Questions Based on the Film

1. Describe how the method of fighting during the Civil War contributed to the

    high casualty rate. _____

    _____

    _____

2. According to Shaw, how are the black troops different from the white troops in

    their use of leisure time and in their attitude? _____

    _____

    _____

3. What is the purpose of the proclamation that Shaw reads from the Confederate

    Congress? _____

    _____

4. Why is flogging so particularly humiliating to Trip?

    _____

    _____

(continued)

Unit 4: The Civil War

Glory (continued)

5. How does the white officer of the contraband troops think secession can be cured?

_____

_____

6. How does the attitude of the white combat troops change towards the 54th Regiment? _____

_____

7. Why do you think the filmmakers chose to call their movie *Glory*?

_____

_____

_____

The West

Teacher's Guide

Dances with Wolves, Orion Pictures, 1990. Directed by Kevin Costner, color, 180 minutes. Distributed on videocassette by Orion Home Video. Nominated for twelve Academy Awards. Film won Best Picture, Best Director, Best Cinematography, and four other Oscars.

Background of the Film

This award-winning film was actor Kevin Costner's first effort as a director. It is a monumental work costing $18 million, which Costner raised partly from overseas investors. The film was a gamble for Orion Pictures, a financially weak studio, and many referred to the movie while it was in production as "Costner's Last Stand."

The logistics of shooting this movie presented an awesome task for the novice director, who had to find and take charge of 3,500 American bison, 300 horses, 2 wolves, 42 wagons, 36 tepees, 500 extras, and 130 crew members. Shooting took 5 months, from July to November, at 27 different locations in South Dakota where temperatures were often over 100 degrees in summer and 20 degrees in late fall. Six months were spent in preproduction and research. To assure historical accuracy, Costner hired an Indian artifact historian, Cathy Smith. Smith was kept on hand for every shot to make certain that the costumes and rituals were correct. The costumes were made using traditional Sioux skills, such as brain tanning (using liquefied animal brains to soften skins) to provide authenticity. Even the war paint was based on traditional designs. Indian artifact restorer Larry Belitz was in charge of creating an 1860's Lakota village with the correct tepees, cooking utensils, and weapons. Even the arrows were made of the same wood—red willow or chokecherry—used by the Sioux. Much of the movie's dialogue is in the Sioux dialect Lakota, with English subtitles. Because none of the Native Americans knew Lakota, they, along with Kevin Costner and Mary McDonnell, were tutored by Doris Leader Charge, an instructor in Lakota studies. One result of the movie has been an increased interest by younger Sioux in learning their tribal language.

This film has been hailed as a major attempt to redress the many erroneous portrayals of American Indians through the years in films and television. Often portrayed either as bloodthirsty savages or half-wits speaking in grunts, Native Americans have been exploited and stereotyped in most of the "old-time" Hollywood Westerns. Costner wanted only Native Americans to portray the Sioux in his film and although not all of the actors used were Lakota, they were all Native Americans. The Sioux are portrayed as real people, making mistakes, laughing, worrying, and making love.

Dances with Wolves has also been hailed as the first "environmental" Western—one that concerns itself with our treatment of nature. The role of animals is particularly noteworthy; they become integral characters in the story. Note particularly that while the Lakota hunt buffalo only to secure their survival needs, they are killed by the encroaching whites not for food, but for their tongues and hides. The wolf who befriends Dunbar is killed by the soldiers for no reason other than sport. The film speaks to the present fouling of the planet as well as examining the past.

This film was not without its detractors. Some critics felt that the film was wrong in portraying all whites, with the exception of Dunbar, as evil, demented, and/or rapacious, and the Indians as the embodiment of virtue. Other critics felt that the film was too "politically correct" in its portrayal of the nineteenth-century frontier; that Dunbar spoke like a twentieth-century political activist transported back to the 1860's and was thus unrealistic for the time the film portrayed.

These criticisms, as well as the many other issues the film itself raises, make this film an excellent springboard for discussion. Treatment of native peoples and their portrayal in media certainly could be one topic. Another topic could be the role of the frontier in American thought and the idea of progress through conquest and expansion, or through unlimited resource exploitation. Frederick Jackson Turner could certainly be used as a source here. *Dances with Wolves* inverts the frontier myth by portraying it as a process of loss and wanton destruction; and the frontier itself not as an empty place awaiting settlement, but as a place inhabited by a people in harmony with its environment, ferociously displaced by ignorant and greedy interlopers who win because of their more powerful weapons of destruction. The myth of "manifest destiny" is a pervasive one in our history and could be examined through the film.

Synopsis of the Plot

The film opens at a Civil War battlefield in Tennessee in 1863. Union soldier John Dunbar has been wounded. Rather than wait to have his leg amputated, he steals a horse and rides unarmed along the no-man's-land between the Union and Confederate lines, tempting fate by challenging the Confederates to fire. He survives and is decorated for heroism. Upon recovering from his wound, he is allowed to pick a new post. Dunbar assigns himself to the furthermost edge of the frontier, because he wants to experience it "before it disappears." But the demented officer who assigns him to Fort Sedgewick and arranges for his transport commits suicide immediately thereafter, and when Dunbar's guide is killed by Indians after dropping him and the outpost's supplies at Fort Sedgewick, there is no one left who knows of Dunbar's posting. When he arrives, he finds the fort is deserted, but he is determined to stay on with only the company of his horse Cisco and a wolf he names Two Socks, with whom the Indians spy him playing. Dunbar rebuilds the fort and cleans up a garbage dump he finds nearby.

Indians visit the fort and attempt to steal Cisco, but are unsuccessful. Dunbar decides to meet with the Indians and establish contact. He comes across a young Indian woman who is hurt. He discovers that she is white. When he brings her to the camp, the Indians tell him to go away—he is not welcome. The Indians decide they should deal with this lone white man. Chief Ten Bears sends Kicking Bird and Wind in His Hair to the fort. The meetings go well. The white woman in the Lakota tribe, whose name is Stands with a Fist, is coaxed into acting as interpreter for Dunbar, although she has not spoken English since she was five years old.

One night, Dunbar wakes to a thundering sound. It is a herd of buffalo. Dunbar rides to the camp to tell the Indians, who immediately move out in search of the herd. The tribe comes across many rotting buffalo carcasses; white hunters have slaughtered them for their skins. When the herd is spotted, the Indians hunt the buffalo for their meat. Dunbar is included in the hunt and the subsequent feasting to celebrate its success. He begins to spend more and more time with the Sioux.

When a Pawnee war party attacks the Sioux camp, Dunbar gets guns and ammunition from the fort to help his friends defend themselves. Dunbar is given an Indian name, "Dances with Wolves," and marries Stands with a Fist in a Sioux wedding ceremony.

The tribe packs and begins to move to winter camp, but Dunbar, in a makeshift costume, half Indian, half soldier, makes one last trip to Fort Sedgewick to retrieve his journal. When he arrives at the fort, he finds it occupied by soldiers. The soldiers shoot Cisco and capture Dunbar, who they presume is a traitor. An illiterate soldier who has found his journal uses its pages as toilet paper. They send Dunbar to Fort Hays to be tried and hanged, but he is rescued by the Sioux and reunited with the tribe. He fears that the soldiers will hunt for him and avenge themselves on the tribe and urges the Indians to move their camp. He and Stands with a Fist leave the tribe to eliminate the threat and when the soldiers do arrive, the Indian camp is deserted.

Note: There may be a longer version of this movie available on videocassette. The book, *Dances with Wolves, The Illustrated Story of the Epic Film,* has a plot synopsis that contains scenes cut during the editing of the film that may be added to the video version.

Ideas for Class Discussion

This unit is an excellent springboard for a discussion about how Native Americans have been portrayed in films and on television. Many films in the past had Indians speaking almost babytalk or in unintelligible grunts. Why do you think this film uses subtitles? How does this affect the viewer and his or her perception of the Lakota people? Related to this might be a discussion of how the Lakota people themselves are portrayed. It is certainly a far cry from the usual portrayal of Native Americans in films—as uncivilized savages. The class might discuss whether this portrayal has swung the pendulum too far in the opposite direction. Another discussion topic is one about the character of John Dunbar and whether he is a 1990's persona in a nineteenth-century setting. Is it likely that a person at that time would be so environmentally aware and sensitive to the virtues of the peoples he encountered?

Books and Materials Relating to This Film and Topic

Brown, Dee. *Bury My Heart at Wounded Knee: An Indian History of the American West* (Henry Holt and Co., 1971).

Connell, Evan S. *Son of the Morning Star: Custer and the Little Bighorn* (North Point Press, 1984). A 1991 two-part, made-for-television movie was based upon this book.

Costner, Kevin, Blake, Michael, and Wilson, Jim. *Dances with Wolves, The Illustrated Story of the Epic Film* (Newmarket Press, 1990).

Friar, Ralph L., and Friar, Natasha. *The Only Good Indian...The Hollywood Gospel* (Drama Book Specialists, 1972).

Other Media Resources for This Time Period

Cheyenne Autumn (1964, 156 minutes, Swank Motion Pictures/Warner Home Video) This film has been compared to *Dances with Wolves* in that it shows the American government's policy of genocide towards Indians.

Little Big Man (1970, 150 minutes, Swank Motion Pictures/Key Video) The sole survivor of Custer's Last Stand relates his life story in both the Indian and white man's worlds.

Unit 5: The West

Dances with Wolves, Orion Pictures, 1990. Directed by Kevin Costner.

Major Character	Actor/Actress
Lieutenant John J. Dunbar	Kevin Costner
Kicking Bird	Graham Greene
Stands with a Fist	Mary Mc Donnell
Wind in His Hair	Rodney A. Grant
Ten Bears	Floyd Red Crow Westerman
Black Shawl	Tantoo Cardinal
Smiles a Lot	Nathan Lee Chasing His Horse
Stone Calf	Jimmy Herman

What to Watch For

Dances with Wolves was produced and directed by Kevin Costner, who also played the part of the main character, John Dunbar. This epic film won seven Academy Awards including Best Picture.

This film has been hailed by many historians as one that redresses many wrongs in Hollywood's portrayal of Native Americans. Costner went to great lengths to provide an accurate picture of Sioux (or, as these people called themselves, Lakota) life. Specialists versed in Sioux culture were hired to make certain that costumes, rituals, and props were authentic. The language spoken by the Sioux in the film with English subtitles is Lakota. A teacher of Lakota studies from Sinte Gloska College in South Dakota worked with crew members, including the native Sioux, to learn Lakota for the film. One result of the popularity of this film has been a renewed interest in the Lakota language and culture by many Sioux.

The film has also been hailed as the first "environmental" Western. Dunbar searches for the unspoiled frontier; he wishes to see it before it is gone. Compare the ways in which the Indians inhabit the land with the ways in which white settlers, soldiers, and hunters occupy it.

Animals play a very important role in the movie. One reason that Costner selected South Dakota as the location for shooting was the proximity of the world's largest privately owned herd of buffalo. Two trained buffalo (Mammoth, owned by rock singer Neil Young, and Cody, the mascot of a meat company) were also used. The scene where a buffalo charges a fallen boy is actually Cody racing toward an Oreo cookie, his favorite treat, held out of camera range by a trainer. The fallen buffalo are wire-framed fur dummies. No animals were harmed in any way to make this film.

This movie has also generated some controversy. Some critics accused Costner of making the Indians too virtuous and the whites too evil. Others felt that Dunbar's sensibilities were those of a twentieth-century person and that the film transferred 1990's values into the world of the 1860's, when the environment was seen simply as a resource to be tamed and exploited for human benefit.

Name _____ Date _____

Unit 5: The West

Dances with Wolves

Vocabulary

Frontier

Garrison

Pawnee

Sioux

Medicine man

Tatonka (buffalo)

Tipi

Questions Based on the Film

1. Why does Dunbar end up at Fort Sedgewick? _____

    _____

    _____

2. What is the significance of Dunbar's discovery of the garbage dump near the

    fort? _____

    _____

    _____

3. Why is Stands with a Fist afraid of Dunbar at first?

    _____

    _____

4. Why has this film been labeled the first "environmental" Western? _____

    _____

    _____

(continued)

Unit 5: The West

Dances with Wolves (continued)

5. How does Dunbar compare the warfare among Indian tribes to the Civil War in which he has participated? _____

_____

_____

6. What kind of helmet does Ten Bears show Dunbar? What are Ten Bears' fears?

_____

_____

7. What devices or techniques does the film use to draw you sympathetically into Lakota life and culture and help you understand the Indian view of the relationship between human beings and their environment? _____

_____

_____

8. Why is Dunbar accused of treason? _____

_____

_____

World War I

Teacher's Guide

1918, Cinecom International Films, 1985. Screenplay by Horton Foote, directed by Ken Harrison, color, 89 minutes. Distributed by Angelika Films and CBS–Fox Video.

Background of the Film

1918 was written by Horton Foote, the Academy Award-winning screenwriter of *To Kill a Mockingbird* and *Tender Mercies*. The film is based on one play from Foote's semiautobiographical nine-play cycle called *The Orphan's Home*, which is about several generations of the Robedaux family in a small town in Texas. *1918* was initially produced as an off-Broadway play with Foote's daughter Hallie playing Elizabeth Robedaux, the role she also plays in the film. Matthew Broderick made his stage debut playing Brother in another play of the cycle (again, the same role he plays in the film).

The film was shot on location in Waxahachie, Texas, where *Places in the Heart* and *Tender Mercies* were filmed. Many local actors and technicians were used, as well as a Dallas-based director who had never worked on a full-length feature film. The final cost of the production was $1.7 million, a very low figure.

The film looks at the impact of two major events on the life of the townspeople of a small town in 1918, the Great War (World War I) and the great influenza pandemic that killed 20 million people worldwide during the fall and winter of 1918–1919—more than the First World War. These events shattered the innocent, optimistic mood of American life. The character of Brother is shown enraptured in the movie house watching glorified scenes of the war while new graves are being dug in the local cemetery. Eventually, even the reality of the war comes home as maimed and shell-shocked soldiers straggle back to the town after the armistice.

Foote wanted to evoke the theme of family and interpersonal relationships in a simpler and less impersonal age. To Foote, the notion of grief and death has become taboo in our contemporary urban world. In a small town, people talked openly about the dead, reminiscing and visiting the graveyards. For example, in the film, Horace becomes obsessed with the location of two family graves and with a desire to know exactly where his ancestors are buried.

The film is historically accurate in the depiction of small-town atmosphere in 1918. The costumes and settings attempt to re-create that time period. Much of the furniture used was taken from Foote's family home in Wharton, Texas. The bedroom set in the Robedaux home was the actual bedroom set that belonged to Foote's parents. The main characters, Horace and Elizabeth, represent Horton Foote's parents.

This movie can be used as a vehicle through which to look at American social history. Such things as entertainment, the role of women, medical science, adoption, and the romantic view of a far-off war are all touched upon. It is a simple, minimalist view of the end of American innocence at a time when outside forces shatter the complacency and optimism of rural, small town America. A "prequel" to this film, *On Valentine's Day* (1986, 106 minutes, Angelika Films/Lorimar Home Video), is set in the same place in 1917.

Synopsis of the Plot

It is autumn, 1918, in Harrison, Texas, and the townspeople are all discussing news from local men who are fighting in Europe. Horace Robedaux shuts his dry goods store and goes to the graveyard to see if there is a stone for his father's grave. He and the cemetery worker discuss the flu epidemic.

At the Robidaux home, Brother visits Elizabeth, his sister. He claims that he wants to join the army. Elizabeth's parents, the Vaughns, come to visit. Papa tells Horace that he is proud that he bought $4,000 worth of war bonds and that if Horace wishes to enlist, the Vaughns will take care of Elizabeth and baby Jenny. Later, Horace confides to Elizabeth that he really doesn't want to join the army.

Brother confides to Elizabeth that he is in trouble. He has lost money gambling, and a girl he has dated is pregnant and wants money for an abortion. Elizabeth gives Brother $200.

More family friends have the flu and one has died. Papa is stricken and Horace also has a fever. In his delirium, Horace thinks that the Germans are attacking them.

As Brother sits alone in the movie house watching scenes of World War I films, the grave diggers are busy as the flu claims more victims.

Horace and Papa eventually recover, but Horace doesn't remember what has happened. Elizabeth tells Horace that she has had the flu and that their baby has died. While they are talking, the town bells ring. Brother bursts in to say that the armistice has been declared.

It is now winter, 1919, and a victory celebration is held for the homecoming troops. Elizabeth, expecting another baby, visits Jenny's grave. The soldiers return a few at a time.

In spring of 1919, Brother is still hanging around; he is finally forced by his father to take a job on a cotton boat. Elizabeth is afraid to have this baby because of what happened to Jenny. Finally, she gives birth to a boy, Horace, Jr. The movie ends with Papa looking at the baby and wondering how the war, the flu, or anything bad could happen to the child. The last shot is of Jenny Robedaux's grave.

Ideas for Class Discussion

1918 could be used as the focus of a discussion on America's growing role as a world power and how this impacts on average American citizens. World War I marks the first time that the United States became a major participant in a conflict with worldwide ramifications. How does war affect ordinary citizens? How are soldiers treated upon their return? How does their experience in war change them? Are the war and the influenza pandemic connected in any way? It might be a good oral history project to see if there are senior citizens in your school district who remember the Great War and the influenza pandemic and can talk about how they were personally affected. The influenza epidemic could be compared with the polio epidemic of the 1940's and early 1950's and the present AIDS epidemic. What are the responses to such epidemics? Do they change human behaviors? (For example, during the polio epidemic, many movie theaters stopped having matinees for children for fear of the disease spreading. During the influenza epidemic of 1918, a private school near Boston held classes outside in tents even in winter because teachers thought fresh air would lessen the risk of contamination.)

Books and Materials Relating to This Film and Topic

Brownlow, Kevin. *The War, the West, and the Wilderness* (Alfred A. Knopf, 1979).

Campbell, Craig W. *Reel America and World War I: A Comprehensive Filmography and History of Motion Pictures in the United States, 1914–1920* (MacFarland, 1985).

Collier, Richard. *The Plague of the Spanish Lady* (Atheneum, 1974).

Devlin, Patrick. *Too Proud to Fight, Woodrow Wilson's Neutrality* (Oxford University Press, 1975).

Ellis, Edward Robb. *Echoes of Distant Thunder, Life in the United States, 1914–1918* (Coward, McCann, and Geoghegan, 1975).

Isenberg, Michael. *War on Film: The American Cinema and World War I, 1914–1941* (Fairleigh Dickinson University Press, 1981).

Other Media Resources for This Period

Civilization (1916, 102 minutes, Video Yesteryear) Thomas Ince's morality play about the immorality of war. Produced while America was still neutral in the war, it contributed to Woodrow Wilson's presidential campaign as the candidate who "kept us out of war." It is a silent era film with printed intertexts and a musical score.

Hearts of the World (1918, 122 minutes, Video Yesteryear/Republic Pictures Home Video) The film made by D.W. Griffith at the request of the British. Griffith got permission to film near the front in France and brought his stars Lillian and Dorothy Gish to shoot scenes there. The resulting footage was not visually exciting enough for American moviegoers and only one short scene was used in the final cut. Griffith and his crew then retreated to southwestern England where the British Army (though desperately short of ammunition) helped him to create the kind of war Americans expected—one with exciting and romantic battles and with clear heroes and villains. This film is silent, with intercards, and a musical score.

Shoulder Arms (1918, 40 minutes, Key Video) Distributed as part of a 119-minute video program that Chaplin himself created in 1958 called *The Chaplin Revue*, which also includes *A Dog's Life* (1918) and *The Pilgrim* (1922). All are silent films with musical scores composed by Chaplin. This is the war comedy that Charlie Chaplin was warned by his friends not to make because the war was too much a holy crusade to make fun of. It was released just before the armistice and became one of the most popular and enduring films of this time. It is filled with wartime conventions and gags and, in an extended dream sequence, Charlie captures Kaiser "Bill." During the war Charlie joined with other Hollywood stars to sell war bonds, and one of the shorts he made for that purpose, called *The Bond* (1918, Reel Images), is also available.

The Big Parade (1925, 126 minutes, Films, Inc./Facets Video) King Vidor's silent antiwar epic, based on Laurence Stallings who served as a marine in the war and lost his leg (as does the movie's hero, played by John Gilbert) at Belleau Wood. The film's re-creation of that battle is truly spectacular.

Wings (1927, 139 minutes, Paramount Home Video) The other silent film classic about the war, this time about the air war. The services of the U.S. Army and Army Air Corps were enlisted by director William Wellman to re-create the Battle of St. Mihiela as the movie's climax. Despite the sound revolution that was taking Hollywood by storm when this film was made, it was *Wings* that won the first Best Picture award.

A Farewell to Arms (1932, 78 minutes, Festival Films/Video Yesteryear) Gary Cooper and Helen Hayes starred in this version of Hemingway's semibiographical novel. An inferior remake appeared in 1957 and is available from Budget Films.

Sergeant York (1940, 134 minutes, McGraw Hill Films/Key Video) The film biography of the World War I Congressional Medal of Honor winner who captured 132 German soldiers almost single-handedly. Telling the story as a pacifist-turned-soldier must be seen as part of the "preparedness" movement that was growing in the United States in 1940. John Huston cowrote the script, Howard Hawks directed, and Gary Cooper (as York) won a Best Actor Academy Award for his performance.

Wilson (1944, 154 minutes, Films, Inc.) Made during World War II, this film portrays the World War I president as an idealist thwarted by shortsighted politicians as he obsessively pursued his vision of a new world order embodied in the League of Nations. The film was meant to be a salutary lesson to Americans about to remake the world after an even more destructive war. It won five Academy Awards but flopped terribly at the box office. Since then, the film has suffered from insensitive cutting and exists in all sorts of edited versions today.

The Cardinal (1953, 175 minutes, Image Enterainment) Otto Preminger's film of Henry Morton Robinson's reverential novel about the trials and growth of an American priest in the context of war, racial and religious bigotry, and the rise of European fascism.

Johnny Got His Gun (1971, 111 minutes, Media Home Entertainment) A depressing film made during the Vietnam War era by once-blacklisted Dalton Trumbo from his 1939 antiwar novel. Timothy Bottoms plays an American soldier who lost his arms, legs, and communications faculties to a German artillery shell and now silently remembers his life from the living tomb of his hospitalized body.

Reds (1981, 200 minutes, Films, Inc./Paramount Home Video) Warren Beatty's biographical film about American radical journalist John Reed and his relationship with Louise Bryant. The film carries us through the tumultuous years of the First World War, the Russian and Bolshevik revolutions, the birth pangs of the American Communist party, and the Russian Civil War, in which Reed died. He was buried in the Kremlin Wall as a hero of the Revolution. The film is not only noteworthy for its spectacle and its passionate commitment, but also for the interviews of Reed's contemporaries (by now in their eighties) that are distributed through it.

There are also a number of excellent documentaries on this period, including:

Goodbye Billy: America Goes to War, 1917–1918 (1972, 25 minutes, Churchill Films and Video) A film made by three historians in association with the American Historical Association's History Education Project.

The Great War (1956, 54 minutes, CRM/McGraw-Hill Films) One of the classic NBC *Project XX* documentaries.

The Great War—1918 (1989, 57 minutes, PBS Video) Part of the PBS *American Experience* series.

Hollywood Goes to War (1980, 54 minutes, HBO Video) This film is Kevin Brownlow and David Gill's *Hollywood: The Silent Years* episode about the war's impact on Hollywood, while *The Moving Picture Boys in the Great War* (1986, 52 minutes, Modern Sound Pictures/Coronet Video) is a documentary about the newsreels narrated by Lowell Thomas.

Homefront 1917-1919: War Transforms American Life (1967, 17 minutes, Films, Inc.) Briefly covers American wartime life and attitudes.

Men of Bronze (1977, 57 minutes, Films, Inc.) The story of the U.S. Army's 369th Infantry Regiment—the unit of African Americans that served longer in action than any other American unit.

The Yanks Are Coming (1974, 52 minutes, Films, Inc.) David Wolper's documentary about America's role in the war.

Unit 6: World War I

1918, Cinecom International Films, 1985. Directed by Ken Harrison, screenplay by Horton Foote.

Major Character	Actor/Actress
Horace Robedaux	William Converse-Roberts
Elizabeth Robedaux	Hallie Foote
Mrs. Vaughn	Rochelle Oliver
Mr. Vaughn	Michael Higgins
Brother	Matthew Broderick
Bessie	Jeannie McCarthy

What to Watch For

In many ways, World War I marked the end of an era for Europe and the United States as well. After several decades of peaceful semi-isolation, America found itself drawn into a world conflict that, as time went on, disillusioned all of the combatants. Brother represents the youthful idealism shown by many towards the war, but note how and where he spends his time. Is the war he witnesses on the screen the real image of what was happening on the European battlefields?

This film looks at victims—victims of a war fought thousands of miles from the small town in Texas that is the scene of the film, and victims of a flu epidemic which killed people on the homefront without regard to age or social standing. The influenza epidemic (or pandemic) of 1918 was of worldwide proportion, killing as many as 20 million people, including 500,000 in this country alone.

The epidemic, coupled with anxieties produced by the war, shook the complacent, optimistic life-style of many Americans. The residents of Harrison, Texas, find themselves seemingly "invaded" by foreign foes: disease, death, and battle scars.

The dress, settings, and furnishings used in this film are accurate for a small town in 1918, and because of this and the fact that the story is based on the experiences of Horton Foote's own family, the film provides a look back at a "slice of American life." Note the emphasis on the cemetery as a center of town life—for example, the visits by families to the graves. In our transient society, this custom is one that has become lost. Note also Horace's fixation on finding out exactly where his father's grave is located, providing his own connection to his family history.

Unit 6: World War I

1918

Vocabulary

Armistice

Influenza

War bonds

Shell shock

Pandemic

Epidemic

Questions Based on the Film

1. Describe small-town life in Texas in 1918. What role does the cemetery play in it?

   _____

   _____

   _____

2. Describe the picture show that Brother attends. _____

   _____

   _____

3. How does Brother explain the flu epidemic? _____

   _____

   _____

4. What does Horace think is happening to him when he is delirious from fever?

   _____

   _____

   _____

(continued)

Unit 6: World War I

1918 (continued)

5. How do the returning veterans bring the reality of the war to the residents of

Harrison, Texas? _____

_____

_____

6. Why is Bessie so afraid? How has the war affected her? _____

_____

_____

Unit 7

The Twenties

Teacher's Guide

Matewan, Cinecom Entertainment Group and Film Gallery, 1987. Directed by John Sayles, color, 100 minutes. Distributed on videocassette by Lorimar Home Video.

Background of the Film

Matewan was both written and directed by John Sayles. It was produced as a low-budget (under $5 million) film independent of any major studio. Despite the drawbacks in trying to "sell" a movie that had an intensely political theme, no rock music, and no upbeat ending, and the problems involved in producing a low-budget movie set in the past and therefore requiring authentic sets and costumes, *Matewan* was a critical success.

Sayles first became interested in writing *Matewan* while hitchhiking through the coal-mining areas of Kentucky and West Virginia. In 1977 he wrote a novel called *Union Dues*. During the course of the research for that book, he came across references to the "Matewan massacre" and to a chief of police in Matewan, West Virginia, named Sid Hatfield, a distant cousin of the Hatfields involved in the legendary feud with the McCoys.

The history of the 1920 Matewan massacre revolves around the efforts of the United Mine Workers to unionize the coal fields of eastern Kentucky and southwestern West Virginia. The United Mine Workers targeted Logan and Mingo Counties to be organized and sent agents into these areas. The mine owners, who had been able to undercut the unionized mines to the north by paying lower wages, were anxious to stop the UMW, an organization that they saw as a creeping disease. Nationwide, public opinion tended to side with the mine operators since, during the Red scare that followed World War I, unions were often equated with the "Bolshevik menace." A strike broke out in Matewan, on the Tug Fort River near the Kentucky border. The mayor of the town, Cabell Testerman, and chief of police, Sid Hatfield, sided with the miners and refused to be bought by the coal company. When agents from the Baldwin-Felts Detective Agency, working for the coal operators, came to evict the miners from company housing, Hatfield confronted them. Shots were fired and, in the ensuing massacre, seven Baldwin-Felts agents, Mayor Testerman, and two miners were killed.

From this basic history, John Sayles fleshed out the story of *Matewan*, using the real characters of Testerman and Hatfield and adding other real, fictional, or composite characters from his research on this period. Few Clothes was a real person, as was the skilled company spy, C.E. Lively. Two main fictional characters are the chief protagonist, the union organizer Joe Kenehan, and the young miner and preacher Danny Radnor. The movie is framed by a narration, which is spoken by Danny as an old man, although we never see him. Sayles decided to focus his movie on the role and effects of violence and, to this end, he made Joe a pacifist. To make him a believable character, Sayles made him a "Wobbly"—a member of the Industrial Workers of the World (IWW), an American union aimed at organizing whole industries rather than individual skilled crafts, as was the contemporary model used by the American Federation of Labor. Historically the IWW, with its promise of uniting all workers into "one big union" and then using general strikes to achieve its objectives, was considered much more of a threat to the American system of business and industry than the AF of L. When the IWW opposed American participation in World War I, government, industry, and the AF of L combined to hound it nearly to extinction. The IWW form of industrywide organizing reemerged in the philosophy of the Congress of Industrial Organizations (CIO) in which the United Mine Workers played a founding role. Danny becomes a convert to Joe's crusade, and afterward he carries on Joe's work.

Many elements of the story are based on fact. Following a long tradition, the coal companies did bring in Italian immigrants and Southern blacks as strikebreakers. The company did own the miners' houses as well as the churches, stores, and just about everything else in the mining towns, and could evict miners without notice or any right of legal redress. Striking miners were forced to set up tent camps after they were evicted from their housing. The references throughout the movie to the union and its organizers as "Reds," "Bolsheviks," or "Communists" are indicative of a time when Red-baiting was effective propaganda for convincing Americans that unions were dangerous and un-American.

Synopsis of the Plot

A narrator sets the time and place—1920 in Matewan, West Virginia. As coal miners learn that the mine operators have brought down the tonnage rate for coal, thereby lowering their wages, they go out on strike. The coal operators bring in black men from Alabama as strikebreakers on the same train to Matewan as Joe Kenehan, an agent sent by the union to organize the miners.

Joe rents a room at Elma Radnor's house; there he meets her son Danny, a trapper boy in the mine and a preacher. Joe is brought to a meeting of the miners at C.E. Lively's Restaurant. The unofficial leader of the black strikebreakers, Few Clothes Johnson, comes to the meeting to make it clear that he is not a scab. Joe urges all the miners to walk out and states that anyone who does will be brought into the union regardless of color or national origin.

In response to the strike the coal operators send two Baldwin-Felts agents, Hickey and Griggs, into town to evict the miners from company housing. Police Chief Sid Hatfield prevents the evictions and deputizes the miners.

When the miners go to confront the black and Italian strikebreakers, the blacks, led by Few Clothes, and the Italians, led by Fausto, throw down their shovels and join the strike. They are welcomed into the union and blacks and whites work together to build a tent camp, since they cannot live in the company housing.

Still in town, the Baldwin-Felts agents try to bribe Sid and the mayor to cooperate. The tent camp is attacked at night and there is a shoot-out between the miners and the coal company guards. One miner is killed and the audience learns that C.E. is a company spy.

To break the miners' trust in Joe, C.E. coerces a young townswoman, Bridey Mae, to say Joe raped her and C.E. tries to show that Joe is a collaborator with the Baldwin-Felts agents. The miners draw straws and Few Clothes is picked to kill Joe. Danny overhears Hickey and Griggs discussing Joe's fate and he preaches a sermon that tells the miners of this treachery. Jace Hilliard, a young mine worker, reaches Few Clothes in time to save Joe's life. The union pulls together once more and Joe is seen doling out strike-relief money.

C.E. tells Turley, the mine manager, that he would like to bring things to a boil. Hilliard is caught stealing coal and Griggs slits his throat on a command from C.E., who then proclaims, "Nothin' like a young boy dyin' to stir things up."

The next day the train brings in a group of Baldwin-Felts men to try once more to carry out evictions in the town. Sid confronts them. A shoot-out takes place between the Baldwin-Felts men, Sid, and the miners. The Felts brothers, Hickey, Griggs, the mayor, and Joe Kenehan are killed.

The narration of the old man comes back in to finish the story. In the last scene we see a lone miner who is shown to be Danny and we realize that the narrator is Danny as an old man who has pledged himself to carry on Joe's mission.

Ideas for Class Discussion

Labor unions in the United States today are often characterized as bloated, corrupt, and bureaucratic special interests. By opening this window to the post-World War I period of labor-management relations, students can explore the nature of industrial and extraction enterprise, the traditional ways in which management exerted control over labor, and the reasons that workers turned to collective bargaining to redress the balance. In the process, the class can discuss the role of government in the economic sector, the alternative modes of labor union organization, the use of political or ideological labels to mark economic self-interest, the ways in which racial and ethnic differences intersected with class interests and were used to prevent unionization, and the role violence played in labor history.

Books and Materials Relating to This Film and Topic

Burns, James MacGregor. *The Workshop of Democracy* (Alfred A. Knopf, 1985).

Carter, Paul Allen. *Another Part of the Twenties* (Columbia University Press, 1977).

Long, Priscilla. *Where the Sun Never Shines: A History of America's Bloody Coal Industry* (Paragon House, 1989).

Phillips, Cabell. "The West Virginia Mine War" (*American Heritage*, August 1974, Vol. XXV, #5, pp. 58–61).

Sayles, John. *Thinking in Pictures: The Making of the Movie "Matewan"* (Houghton-Mifflin, 1987).

Other Media Resources for This Time Period

The Court Martial of Billy Mitchell (1955, 100 minutes, Kit Parker Films/Republic Pictures Home Video) Deals with the struggle over military preparedness and the role of air power during the traditionalist and isolationist mood of the 1920's.

Eight Men Out (1988, 119 minutes, Swank Motion Pictures/Orion Home Video) A John Sayles film about the 1919 Chicago "Black Sox" baseball scandal.

The Great Gatsby (1974, 146 minutes, Films, Inc./Paramount Home Video) A look at the Roaring Twenties of the well-to-do through the eyes of its greatest literary character, F. Scott Fitzgerald.

Inherit the Wind (1960, 127 minutes, Films Inc./Evergreen Video Society; Laser Disc version is available from Image Entertainment) The film version of the Jerome Lawrence/Robert E. Lee play about the 1925 Scopes "Monkey Trial" that pitted evolutionary theory against the authority of the Bible, and Clarence Darrow (Spencer Tracy) against William Jennings Bryan (Fredric March).

Sacco and Vanzetti (1971, 120 minutes, Kit Parker Films/United Home Video) An Italian film with English dubbed in that investigates the 1921 trial and eventual execution of the two Italian immigrants on charges of robbery and murder—charges that many believe resulted from their anarchist politics rather than their guilt.

The Spirit of St. Louis (1957, 137 minutes, Kit Parker Films/Warner Home Video) The story of America's greatest hero, Charles A. Lindbergh, in a decade that exalted heroes.

Unit 7: The Twenties

Matewan, Cinecom Entertainment Group and Film Gallery, 1987. Directed by John Sayles.

Major Character	**Actor/Actress**
Joe Kenehan	Chris Cooper
Few Clothes Johnson	James Earl Jones
Danny Radnor	Will Oldham
Elma Radnor	Mary McDonnell
Sid Hatfield	David Strathairn
C.E. Lively	Bob Gunton
Bridey Mae	Nancy Mette
Hilliard Elkins	Jace Alexander
Hickey	Kevin Tighe
Griggs	Gordon Clapp
Mayor Cabell Testerman	Josh Mostel

What to Watch For

This film is based on a true event: the so-called "Matewan massacre" of 1920, a shoot-out between gunmen of the Baldwin-Felts Detective Agency, working for the mine owners, and striking miners. The police chief, Sid Hatfield, and the mayor of Matewan, Cabell Testerman, sided with the miners—an unusual occurrence at a time when mining towns were owned and controlled by the coal operators.

In most historical films, the events and characters are "telescoped"; the time span is cut down and the number of characters reduced to make the story easier to comprehend. Sayles, however, has added characters and stretched events out. His two main characters, union organizer Joe Kenehan, and young miner Danny Radnor, are fictional characters, added to help tell a story. Joe and Danny *could* have existed; they conform to the attitudes and personalities of that time and place. Interestingly, Few Clothes Johnson, the leader of the black miners brought in as strikebreakers, was a real person who Sayles discovered while researching the topic of Matewan.

The unionization of the coalfields of eastern Kentucky and southwestern West Virginia was a bloody chapter in U.S. labor history. This movie portrays many of the issues of that struggle. Note how the coal companies exert economic control over the miners, as in the scene where the mine manager is going over company rules and so-called "benefits" with the newly hired black miners. Note also the popular prejudices against unions and union activities as expressed by the hard-shell preacher and the Baldwin-Felts agents. Popular opinion in the United States was on the side of the coal operators, who wanted to prevent the United Mine Workers union from entering the coalfields.

Unit 7: The Twenties

Matewan

Vocabulary

Bolshevik

Wobblies

Scab

UMW

Company store

Questions Based on the Film

1. What are the miners' complaints against the mine owners that have led them to go on strike? _____

    _____

    _____

2. How does the coal operator in Matewan exert an economic hold on the miners? (*Hint:* Think of the scene where Turley explains company policies to the newly hired black miners.) _____

    _____

    _____

3. What is the role of music in the film? How is it used to set the mood or tell a story? _____

    _____

4. Why is there, on the part of so many, a suspicion against unions during this time in American history? _____

    _____

    _____

5. After Hilliard's death, what are Danny's arguments against Joe's pacifism and the union? _____

    _____

    _____

The Great Depression

Teacher's Guide

The Grapes of Wrath, Twentieth Century-Fox, 1940. Directed by John Ford, black and white, 129 minutes. Distributed on videocassette by CBS-Fox Video and available from Zenger Video. John Ford won an Oscar for Best Director. Jane Darwell won an Oscar for Best Supporting Actress.

Background of the Film

The Great Depression was one of the most devastating events in American history and nowhere was the impact more poignant than among the small farmers of the Great Plains. Overfarming, poor land use, depressed agricultural prices, absentee landlords, and long-term drought had caused the South Central States to become the Dust Bowl. Thousands of sharecroppers and small farmers (known as "Okies" or "Arkies," depending on their home state) were thrown off or blown off the land with virtually nowhere to go. Many were lured to California by the promise of agricultural jobs in the rich valleys of the "Golden State."

John Steinbeck's Pulitzer Prize-winning novel about a family of sharecroppers from Oklahoma trying to find work and stay together as a family unit became an immediate classic. Darryl F. Zanuck of Twentieth Century-Fox bought the movie rights to the book for $75,000—the highest price paid for any novel of the 1930's, even exceeding the amount paid for *Gone With the Wind*. The movie almost immediately became the subject of much controversy. At first Zanuck was accused of delaying production of the movie because of pressure from business and agricultural interests and Oklahoma and California state officials. When shooting did begin, Zanuck was accused of softening the desolate picture Steinbeck had portrayed of the migrant Okies. Then, when the film was finally shown to be sensitive to the tragic plight of the migrants, mainstream critics objected to the picture, or any picture having such a bleak message and not providing pure entertainment. Others, particularly on the left, objected to the glossing over of the economic sources of the evil. One critic, Ernest L. Mayers, did defend Zanuck, pointing out that if there could not be films with a message, that would leave room for mysteries, fairy tales, thin men, and the two Mickeys—Rooney and Mouse. (*Fifty Classic Motion Pictures*, David Zinman. Chelsea House, 1983, p. 190.)

Ultimately, the film was a commercial success; however, even though it has come to be regarded as a film classic, it remains controversial in many ways. Many critics continue to feel that Ford changed the radical political and economic nature of Steinbeck's novel into a more politically conservative story in which the major emphasis is on the strength and perseverance of the American family. Instead of images that reflect the land and the social conditions of the time, most of the visual images revolve around the Joad family. Most of the film was shot indoors or on a studio lot, with many views of the Joads and other Okies taking on the appearance of tableaus reflecting popular iconography of the Depression as seen in the photographs of Walker Evans or Dorothea Lange. Teachers might wish to use these photos with this film as a good supplementary source.

Synopsis of the Plot

The movie begins with a graphic explaining the Dust Bowl and that this is the story of one family's experience. The scene then opens with Tom Joad walking along a country road in Oklahoma. He has just been paroled from the penitentiary after serving four years for homicide. On his way to the family home he meets Casy, a preacher, who tells him that there is much to preach about now. Tom finds his family home deserted. He meets Muley, a sharecropper like himself, who tells Tom that his family is at Uncle John's house and that everyone is being forced off the land. The caterpillar tractor has replaced the sharecropper; one tractor can do the work of fourteen farmers. Tom finds his family preparing to leave for California, where a handbill has advertised good pay for 800 fruit pickers. The family of twelve loads up the old Hudson truck and heads west on Route 66 with their life savings of $150.

The trip is too much for the old people; Grampa suffers a stroke and dies. He is buried by the roadside, whereTom leaves a note saying: "This here is Willeam James Joad, dyed of a stroke, old, old man. His folks buried him because they got no money to pay for funerals. Nobody killed him, just a stroke and he dyed." When the family stops for the night at a camp, they meet a man who has been to California and he warns them that there are no jobs. Granma dies during the desert crossing, but Ma pretends that Granma is merely sick in order to get quickly through the agricultural inspectors at the California border.

The Joads arrive at a camp crowded with Okies all looking for work. As Ma is cooking, she is surrounded by dozens of starving children. A work contractor comes to the camp to recruit workers, but won't say what the wage is. A fight breaks out and a deputy kills a woman bystander. Tom trips the deputy before he can fire again and then flees to avoid capture. Casy is taken away as an agitator. The Joad family flees the camp upon learning that people from a nearby town are planning to burn it down.

The Joads get a job at the Keene Ranch picking peaches for five cents a box. The conditions are poor and the ranch is surrounded by angry workers. Tom meets Casy who tells him that some workers are on strike and urges Tom to come out and join to keep the price up. While they are meeting, a group of guards attacks and kills Casy. Tom kills a guard, but is marked across the face. The Joad family escapes the farm at night while hiding Tom.

The family finally checks into a camp run by the Department of Agriculture. The camp is run democratically by the workers themselves and the conditions are dramatically different from the previous camp. Still, there is hostility toward the Okies, and the camp is warned that there will be trouble at the Saturday night dance. Deputies move in, but the camp members have defused any problems. Later that night Tom wakes to hear two policemen checking his license number; he realizes that they are on his trail. Tom knows that to protect his family, he must leave. In his farewell to Ma, Tom vows to carry on Casy's fight.

The Joads hear of work in Fresno and push on, always hoping for something better. Ma keeps them together; the film ends with her exclamation: "We're the people that live. Can't wipe us out. Can't lick us. We'll go on forever. 'Cause we're the people."

Ideas for Class Discussion

Of course, to read Steinbeck's novel would be an ideal way to approach this film. How faithful is the film to the original mood and story line of the book? The farmers of the Dust Bowl present an indelible image of the Depression for many Americans, but what were the experiences of people in other parts of the country? It is strongly recommended that teachers show the short documentary *The Plow That Broke the Plains* in conjunction with the showing of *The Grapes of Wrath.*

Books and Materials Relating to This Film and Topic

Bonnifield, Paul. *The Dust Bowl: Men, Dirt and Depression* (University of New Mexico Press, 1979).

French, Warren. *Filmguide to* The Grapes of Wrath (Bloomington: Indiana University Press, 1973).

Hurt, Douglas. *The Dust Bowl: An Agricultural and Social History* (Nelson Hall, 1981).

Rollins, Peter C. *Hollywood as Historian* (University Press of Kentucky, 1983).

Steinbeck, John. *The Grapes of Wrath* (1939).

Zinman, David. *Fifty Classic Motion Pictures* (Chelsea House, 1983).

Other Media Resources for This Time Period

Bonnie and Clyde (1967, 111 minutes, Films, Inc./Warner Home Video) The story of a group of bank robbers who terrorized the Midwest in the 1930's and became tragic folk heroes. Note that the choreographed violence in the film is quite graphic, especially at the end.

The Color Purple (1985, 152 minutes, Swank Motion Pictures/Warner Home Video) Starring Whoopie Goldberg, this film is about black survival in the Depression-age South.

Our Daily Bread (1934, 71 minutes, Kit Parker Films or MOMA/Nelson Entertainment) A classic dealing with the effects of the Depression and the attempt of some displaced urbanites to "return to the land" and start an agricultural cooperative.

Places in the Heart (1984, 102 minutes, Films, Inc./CBS–Fox Video) A film about agricultural survival and social tolerance in Waxahachie, Texas, during the Depression.

The Plow That Broke the Plains (1936, 26 minutes, National Audio Visual Center) Pare Lorentz's classic documentary sponsored by the New Deal's Resettlement Administration. A version that restores the film's original ending that advertised New Deal agencies and caused a furor in Congress, along with a frame-by-frame commentary and a set of source materials related to the film, is available as part of the *Image As Artifact* video package from the American Historical Association.

The Sting (1973, 129 minutes, Swank Motion Pictures/MCA Home Video) Paul Newman film that reflects the mood of Depression-era America.

To Kill a Mockingbird (1963, 129 minutes, Swank Motion Pictures/MCA Home Video) The classic story of a six-year-old growing up in a small Southern town and confronting racial bigotry.

Unit 8: The Great Depression

The Grapes of Wrath, Twentieth Century-Fox, 1940, directed by John Ford.

Major Character	**Actor/Actress**
Tom Joad	Henry Fonda
Ma Joad	Jane Darwell
Casy	John Carradine
Pa Joad	Russell Simpson
Grampa	Charley Grapewin
Granma	Zeffie Tilbury
Muley	John Qualen

What to Watch For

Based on John Steinbeck's Pulitzer Prize-winning novel of 1939, this film has become a classic in its own right.

The Great Depression was a devastating event in twentieth-century America and this film chronicles its effect on the Joad family of Oklahoma. Poor farming practices and an extended drought turned the south central states into the Dust Bowl. Lured by the promise of jobs and good pay, thousands of "Okies," like the Joads, loaded up their jalopies and made the trek to California. What they find in the "Promised Land" is that the overabundance of labor and shortage of jobs has led the growers to slash wages to near-starvation levels.

The film takes place in 1933, the depths of the Great Depression. Note how the Joads and other families lose their land and homes. Also note the conditions that await them in California in the labor camps.

It is important for you to know that this film has been the continuing subject of controversy. Many critics felt that the harsh indictments in Steinbeck's novel were softened in the film and that the director focused too much on one family, the Joads, and their struggle to keep together as a unit, rather than on the more universal theme of the economic and political inequities of this time period. Other critics felt that this film had too much of a "message" and not enough entertainment value. What do you think about the purpose of films in general and whether their only function is to entertain?

Unit 8: The Great Depression

The Grapes of Wrath

Vocabulary

Dust Bowl
Okies
Migrant worker
Sharecropper
Homicide

Questions Based on the Film

1. According to Muley, what makes his land belong to him? _____

   _____

2. Contrast the superintendent or land agent with the sharecroppers as he comes to
   tell them to leave the land. _____

   _____

   _____

3. How are the Joads helped at the roadside diner in New Mexico? _____

   _____

4. What is the reaction of the service station attendants to the Okies before they set
   out across the desert? _____

   _____

5. Why are the Okies met with hostility and suspicion by the native Californians?

   _____

   _____

   _____

6. Contrast the camp at the Keene Ranch with the Farmworker's Wheat Patch
   Camp. _____

   _____

World War II

Teacher's Guide

Air Force, Warner Brothers, 1943. Directed by Howard Hawks, black and white, 124 minutes. Distributed on videocassette by MGM–UA Home Video and available from Facets Video.

Background of the Film

Starting with the historical fact that a squadron of B-17's arrived in Hawaii during the Japanese attack on Pearl Harbor, *Air Force* traces the adventures of one fictional bomber crew across the Pacific to the Philippines, to the Battle of the Coral Sea, to a crash landing on an Australian beach. The movie received help from the Army Air Corps because General Hap Arnold saw the need for a movie that would show the American people the Air Force in action. In writing the script, Dudley Nichols had at his disposal battle reports supplied by the War Department and the technical advice of Captain Samuel Triffy, an Air Corps pilot. The plot, which grew out of the collaboration of Nichols, Triffy, and director Howard Hawks, proved to be little more than a vehicle for portraying the Air Force winning the war almost single-handedly.

Air Force in fact anticipated history, sometimes by months, sometimes by years. The climactic air-sea battle, created with miniatures and special effects, might have borne a vague resemblance to the Battles of the Coral Sea and Midway. But it had been staged and filmed before the actual battles had taken place. B-17's did participate in both actions, although not in the manner portrayed in the film.

Despite its mythical-cum-historical narrative, *Air Force* did more than entertain the American people. The movie slaughter of the Japanese fleet provided a catharsis for the setbacks suffered at Pearl Harbor, Wake Island, and the Philippines. Tied into the plot were continuous overt and subtle propaganda messages, conveyed in terms that were becoming familiar to wartime moviegoers. The crew of the *Mary Ann* consisted of a heterogeneous cross section of the nation except for an African American.

The crew is diverse and fractious, but against all others its members unite, take care of each other, and everyone does his assigned job for the good of the plane.

In contrast, the Japanese are all characterized as sneaky and treacherous and throughout the film are referred to in derogatory terms. This message is constantly reinforced beginning with the opening scenes. On the way to Hawaii, the crew hears a news broadcast that a Japanese peace envoy was planning to meet with Secretary of State Hull on the morning of December 7. When the plane lands at Pearl Harbor, the crew is immediately told of Japanese sabotage of American planes before the attack (historically untrue). The Japanese are portrayed as fighting unfairly, attacking without warning, and shooting at a helpless flier as he parachutes from his disabled plane. Not only were the Japanese evil, but they were shown as inferior in fair combat. The *Mary Ann* shoots down Japanese plane after plane, and the Air Force sinks the entire enemy fleet.

The message stands out clearly: The United States will win the war; we may have lost the first round through deceit, but victory will be ours. The movie's prophecy of victory, repeated enough times, would inevitably have a positive influence on the war effort.

Synopsis of the Plot

On the evening of December 6, 1941, the *Mary Ann*, a B-17 bomber, takes off on a training mission to Hawaii. As the plane travels across the Pacific, the ethnic and geographic diversity of the crew is emphasized, as is the estrangement of one of its members (Sergeant Winocki) from the service. The crew of the plane learns of the Japanese attack on Pearl Harbor and the *Mary Ann* is diverted to a small emergency landing field. The plane is attacked by fifth columnists; the *Mary Ann* takes off and lands at Hickam Field, where the evidence of the Japanese attack is still very apparent.

The crew next receives orders to fly to the Philippines by way of Wake Island. They are joined by Lieutenant Tex Rader, a fighter pilot who is being assigned to Manila. The friendly rivalry between bomber and fighter crews is shown in the conversation en route. The *Mary Ann* arrives at Wake Island where a small number of U.S. marines are preparing for a defense against a much larger Japanese force. The only passenger the plane picks up at Wake Island is a dog named Tripoli, who goes into a rage at the mention of Tojo's name.

When the bomber arrives in the Philippines, they hear accounts of how the Americans are outnumbered, but still are superior fighters to the Japanese. The crew chief, White, learns that his son has been killed. The *Mary Ann* takes off to avoid a Japanese air strike and goes in search of the invasion fleet. Instead, the B-17 runs into a squadron of Japanese planes and, in a display of American superiority, shoots down plane after plane. Vastly outnumbered, the bomber receives numerous hits and the pilot, Quincannon, is mortally wounded. The crew bails out except for Winocki who belly-lands the plane at Clark Field.

The crew arrives back at the base to be by Quincannon's bedside when he dies. They promise to repair the *Mary Ann* and have the plane fly once more. In a race to become airborne before the Japanese arrive, the crew works on the bomber. Private Chester volunteers to fly as a tail gunner on an observation plane. When his plane is hit by a Japanese zero, he parachutes and is machine-gunned to death in a dramatic display of Japanese treachery and barbarism. At the very last minute while the enemy reaches the airfield, the *Mary Ann*, now piloted by Rader, takes off and heads towards Australia.

When the *Mary Ann* comes upon the Japanese fleet, the bomber radios the information to Allied air bases and ships. When a huge formation of American planes arrives, the *Mary Ann* leads them in the attack, slaughtering the Japanese fleet. Short of fuel, the *Mary Ann* is forced to crash-land in the surf on a beach in Australia. The closing scene shows the surviving crew members preparing to attack Tokyo with a squadron of bombers, an event that historically did not begin until 1944.

Ideas for Class Discussion

This film lends itself to a discussion of propaganda. What is and isn't propaganda? Is this film a piece of propaganda? What elements of it can be identified as propagandistic? And is propaganda ever justified? The crew of the *Mary Ann* represents the archetypal American melting pot of the World War II era. Almost every World War II combat film that dwelt on a small combat unit mirrored that composition. Its composition, and what groups are missing from it, make an excellent discussion topic. It also might prove productive to discuss the internment of the Japanese during World War II and the attitudes that are portrayed in A*ir Force*.

Books and Materials Relating to
This Film and Topic

Blum, John Morton. *V Was for Victory: Politics and American Culture During World War II* (Harcourt Brace Jovanovich, 1976).

Dower, John W. W*ar Without Mercy: Race and Power in the Pacific War* (Pantheon, 1987).

Fussell, Paul. *Wartime: Understanding and Behavior in the Second World War* (Oxford University Press, 1989).

Koppes, Clayton R., and Black, Gregory D. *Hollywood Goes to War* (The Free Press, 1987).

Orriss, Bruce W. *When Hollywood Ruled the Skies* (Aero Associates, 1984).

Schaffer, Ronald. *Wings of Judgment: American Bombing in World War II* (Oxford University Press, 1985).

Suid, Lawrence Howard, ed. *Air Force* (University of Wisconsin Press, 1983).

———— *Guts and Glory, Great American War Movies.* Addison Wesley, 1978.

Terkel, Studs. *The Good War: An Oral History of World War II* (Pantheon, 1984).

Other Media Resources for This Time Period

The Battle of the Bulge (1965, 141 minutes, Kit Parker Films/Warner Home Video) A workmanlike telling of the stopping of the last desperate German offensive. The video has been unfortunately cut by 23 minutes, making the story less intelligible than it was originally.

A Bridge Too Far (1977, 175 minutes, Films, Inc./CBS–Fox Video) Sir Richard Attenborough's careful (some say at the expense of dramatic impact) reconstruction of Operation Market Garden. It is based on Cornelius Ryan's last book.

Fat Man and Little Boy (1989, 126 minutes, Films, Inc./Paramount Home Video) The somewhat fictionalized story of the Manhattan Project—the building of the atomic bomb—with Paul Newman as General Leslie Groves, the military engineer and builder of the Pentagon who was given the job of producing a nuclear weapon before the Germans did.

Ike: The War Years (1978, 196 minutes, Zenger Video) The edited version of a six-hour television miniseries starring Robert Duvall. Its central events are the D-day invasion and Ike's "romance" with his driver Kay Summersby (played by Lee Remick).

The Longest Day (1962, 180 minutes, Films, Inc./CBS–Fox Video) Darryl Zanuck's epic all-star recreation of the D-day invasion. It was the first of these docudramas and some think the best.

MacArthur (1978, 130 minutes, Swank Motion Pictures/MCA Home Video) Gregory Peck plays the controversial general, from his assumption of military command in the Pacific to his firing by President Truman, in a film that takes a middle course between genius and megalomania in assessing his character.

Memphis Belle (1990, 106 minutes, Swank Motion Pictures/Warner Home Video) The composite and partly fictional story of a single B-17 crew as it prepares for and carries out its last mission over Europe. It is based on William Wyler's wartime composite documentary of the same title, which is also available on film and video (42 minutes, Burbank Video).

Midway (1977, 135 minutes, Swank Motion Pictures/MCA Home Video) The epic "all-star" reconstruction of the carrier battle that ended the Japanese expansion in the Pacific. The version available on video leaves out the Battle of the Coral Sea section that provides essential background to the Midway decisions and leaves in the fictional (and silly) Charlton Heston love story.

Patton (1970, 171 minutes, Films, Inc./CBS–Fox Video) Features George C. Scott's riveting and troubling portrayal of the general, from North Africa to his death.

PT 109 (1963, 140 minutes, Kit Parker Films/Warner Home Video) The story of John F. Kennedy's service during World War II, based on Kennedy's own account. Cliff Robertson was chosen with the approval of the president to play him. Since Kennedy's death, questions about this episode have arisen among historians, but none of this is reflected in the film.

They Were Expendable (1945, 136 minutes, Films, Inc./MGM–UA Home Video) John Ford's personal version of the PT squadrons that harried the Japanese invasion of the Philippines in early 1942. It starred Robert Montgomery and John Wayne.

To Hell and Back (1965, 196 minutes, Swank Motion Pictures/MCA Home Video) The sanitized autobiographical film about (and starring) Audie Murphy, who was America's most decorated soldier in World War II, receiving twenty-four medals for valor, including the Congressional Medal of Honor.

Tora, Tora, Tora (1970, 161 minutes, Films, Inc./CBS–Fox Video) An American-Japanese coproduction about the bombing of Pearl Harbor.

Twelve O'Clock High (1949, 132 minutes, CBS–Fox Video) The story of the war toll as a result of ordering young men to their deaths in the first high-risk days of the American daylight bombing campaign over Europe. Gregory Peck plays General Frank Savage and Dean Jagger his adjutant, Major Harvey Stoval. Jagger won an Oscar for his performance.

In addition to these, there are documentaries on specific aspects of the war as it affected American life. The best of these include *The Homefront* (1985, 90 minutes, Churchill Films and Video) available in three parts with a companion book; *The Life and Times of Rosie the Riveter* (1980, 65 minutes, Clarity Education Productions/Direct Video); *Silver Wings and Santiago Blue* (1984, 88 minutes, PBS Video) about women pilots during World War II; *A Question of Loyalty* (1982, 50 minutes, Ambrose Video) and *Nisei Soldier* (1984, 30 minutes, Fox Video) both about the wartime internment on the U.S. West Coast of Americans of Japanese ancestry.

Unit 9: World War II

Air Force, Warner Brothers, 1943. Directed by Howard Hawks.

Major Character	Actor/Actress
Captain Mike Quincannon	John Ridgely
Lieutenant Bill Williams	Gig Young
Lieutenant Tommy McMartin	Arthur Kennedy
Lieutenant Monk Hauser	Charles Drake
Sergeant Robby White	Harry Carey
Corporal Weinberg	George Tobias
Corporal Peterson	Ward Wood
Private Chester	Ray Montgomery
Sergeant Joe Winocki	John Garfield
Lieutenant Tex Rader	James Brown

What to Watch For

Air Force was a major box office success and a great morale-builder for Americans during World War II. After the Japanese attack on Pearl Harbor and rapid conquest of the Pacific, Americans needed to hear and see a message of hope; *Air Force* provided this.

Watch for examples of propaganda throughout the entire film such as the constantly repeated theme that America will eventually win the war. Through treachery and deceit on the part of the Japanese, America has lost the first round, but in a fair fight, we will persevere and victory will ultimately be ours.

The movie is a blend of truth and fiction. Japanese fifth columnists (enemy sympathizers who sabotage within a country) *did not* damage any planes in Hawaii. The air-sea battle was created with miniatures and filmed *before* the Battles of the Coral Sea and Midway had taken place. Regular bombing raids of Japan *did not* begin until 1944 and were carried out by B-29 Super Fortresses, not the B-17's as portrayed in the film.

Note how the Japanese are all characterized as sneaky and treacherous and throughout the film are referred to in derogatory terms. They have been successful because they do not fight fair, but the film shows the Americans are superior in combat. Remember when this film was produced and what was happening in the world. This film was produced with the help of the Army Air Corps to bolster morale and contribute to the war effort.

Name _____   Date _____

Unit 9: World War II

Air Force

Vocabulary

B-17 bomber   Pearl Harbor

Bombardier   "Rising Sun"

Fifth column   Sabotage

Mr. Moto

Questions Based on the Film

1. What characteristics do Americans display in the film? How do these characteristics combine to ensure an American victory in a fair fight? _____

    _____

    _____

2. According to the film, why is the attack on Pearl Harbor particularly treacherous?

    _____

    _____

3. Give three examples from the film that were meant to portray the Japanese as deceitful and winning by unfair fighting. _____

    _____

    _____

4. Why do the marines give their dog to the crew of the *Mary Ann*?

    _____

    _____

    _____

5. In a paragraph, explain how this film might have contributed to American morale during World War II. _____

    _____

    _____

The Cold War

Teacher's Guide

Dr. Strangelove or: How I Learned to Stop Worrying and Love the Bomb, Columbia Pictures, 1964. Written, produced, and directed by Stanley Kubrick, black and white, 93 minutes. Distributed by RCA–Columbia Pictures Home Video.

Background of the Film

Hollywood had almost always portrayed the United States military as infallible and heroic (see, for example, *Air Force*). This changed in the early 1960's, particularly after the nuclear war scare and peaceful solution of the Cuban missile crisis, when the cold war appeared to be thawing. Also, new producers and directors had appeared during the 1950's who were socially conscious, not dependent upon the military for any assistance, and thus could make antiestablishment movies. The atomic bomb and its use as a nuclear threat became a topic for several movies that portrayed the military and nuclear brinkmanship in a very critical light. Stanley Kubrick's film is one of these. Kubrick had previously directed the antiwar film *Paths of Glory* (1958) about French Army mutinies during World War I, and had directed *Spartacus* (1960) about the Roman slave revolt. *Dr. Strangelove*, which he wrote, produced, and directed, is one of the best-known of these movies. Kubrick would go on to write, produce, and direct *2001: A Space Odyssey* in 1969, *A Clockwork Orange* in 1971, and *Full Metal Jacket* in 1987.

Dr. Strangelove was suggested to Kubrick by the novel *Red Alert* by Peter George, a thriller about an accidental nuclear attack. Originally, Kubrick's movie was to be a serious suspense film, but he found satire or "black comedy" was the best way to tell the story and make his point. Black comedy is comedy that walks a fine line between horror and humor, where things are so serious that laughter is the only way to break the tension.

Since the military often provided technical assistance and material resources to film producers making war movies, Kubrick actually approached the U.S. Air Force to discuss the film. In this instance, the Air Force refused to provide any cooperation, based not only on the film's proposed portrayal of its officers as deranged and ludicrous, but on what the Pentagon regarded as the misrepresentation of the Positive Control safeguards against an accidental or unauthorized nuclear attack. According to the Air Force, General Ripper's one-man decision to launch a nuclear assault on the Soviet Union would be impossible because an SAC (Strategic Air Command) officer cannot order such an attack. Only the president has the attack code which is relayed to SAC headquarters. According to the military, this system was "fail-safe"; it could not be subverted. Kubrick did much research on the subject and disagreed that it was fail-safe.

Several historians believe that *Dr. Strangelove* strikes at some commonly held attitudes of the cold war era: American anti-Communist paranoia, blind faith in modern technology, and the lack of a true understanding of the enormity of a nuclear war. (See for example Charles Maland's article "Dr. Strangelove: Nightmare Comedy and the Ideology of Liberal Consensus," in Peter C. Rollins's *Hollywood as Historian*, University of Kentucky Press, 1983.) The character of Ripper satirizes the cold war paranoia towards communism that even regarded the fluoridation of water as a Communist conspiracy. *Dr. Strangelove* appears as a bizarre composite of nuclear theorists. Many filmgoers identified him as a composite of army missile project director Wernher von Braun, and nuclear war theorists Herman Kahn and Henry Kissinger. Major King Kong's speech to his crew is more like a traditional World War II pep talk than a speech appropriate for someone about to participate in the destruction of the world. Note also the survival kit each crewman receives and the irony of worrying about such things in event of a nuclear war.

This is a complex movie in many ways with numerous examples of satire and possible innuendos. Is, for example, President Muffley supposed to be reminiscent of Democratic liberal Adlai Stevenson? There have been numerous articles written about the film, particularly in the 1980's. When it was released, *Dr. Strangelove* received mixed reviews that ranged from those attacking it as a disservice to the nation to those praising it as the best American film in years. An interesting side note is that when SAC commander General Curtis LeMay found out about *Dr. Strangelove*, he encouraged the making of the Rock Hudson film *A Gathering of Eagles* to show that Air Force officers were competent and that fail-safe safeguards did exist to prevent an accidental or unauthorized attack like that portrayed in Kubrick's film. It is also interesting to note that there were three other "doomsday" films produced at around the same time: *Fail Safe* (1964), based on the Eugene Burdick and Harvey Wheeler novel; *Seven Days in May* (1964), from a Rod Serling script about a military coup to prevent peace being made with Russia; and *The Bedford Incident* (1965), based on a novel by Mark Rascovich, about an unintended nuclear exchange at sea. All of these are available on videocassette.

Synopsis of the Plot

The action opens at Turpleson Air Force Base when British liaison officer Group Captain Mandrake receives a phone call from Air Force General Ripper that he is putting the base on condition Red. The scene then cuts to a B-52 bomber where a top-secret coded message comes through ordering the aircraft to attack Russia. The pilot, Major Kong, can't believe the message and asks for a confirmation of the order.

At General Turgidson's "love nest" in Washington, a phone call comes through that an attack plan has been put into effect and General Ripper has sealed off the base. On board Major Kong's plane, the crew members prepare for the attack and open their secret orders. At the base, Mandrake questions Ripper's orders.

At the Pentagon in the War Room, the president is meeting with Turgidson and other commanders. Turgidson tries to explain what has happened and excitedly points out its possibilities. Instead, the Russian Ambassador de Sadesky, wearing a hidden camera, is brought into the War Room and the president contacts Premier Kissov on the hot line. The president tells the premier about the attack and advises him to shoot the American bombers down since they cannot be recalled. The premier tells the ambassador about the existence of a "doomsday machine," which is programmed to automatically respond to any aggression by detonating nuclear weapons which will make the earth uninhabitable for ninety-nine years. The ambassador relays this to the president and officers.

Back at the base, an army unit, led by Colonel Guano, is trying to break through base security forces. Ripper tells Mandrake that the Communists are involved in a plot to poison the world by fluoridation. When the Air Force security troops surrender, Mandrake tries to coax Ripper into telling him the recall code. Ripper shoots himself.

The planes are rapidly approaching their targets. Kong's plane is hit by a missile, but the pilot is able to continue on despite the damage.

At the base, Mandrake is confronted by Colonel Guano. Mandrake tries to convince him that he knows the recall code and must call the president. Eventually, Mandrake gets through via a pay phone (finding change for the phone causes a confrontation between Mandrake and Guano), and all the planes are recalled except for Kong's plane, which does not receive the message since its radio is damaged. As the plane approaches the target, it is discovered that the bomb doors won't open. Kong climbs onto the bomb, gets the doors to open, and rides the bomb to its target.

Back in the War Room, Dr. Strangelove recommends that everyone move to a deep mine shaft for one hundred years to survive the radioactivity released by the doomsday machine. With growing excitement, he speaks of a new master race and, as if by uncontrollable reflex, reverts to his Nazi roots. The movie ends as mushroom clouds appear and the song "We'll Meet Again Someday" plays.

Ideas for Class Discussion

With the end of the cold war and the gradual "builddown" of nuclear weapons, a film like *Dr. Strangelove* may seem a bit old-fashioned to students. But the issue of who controls the button that might unleash global destruction is still vital and perhaps more complex now than it was in the bipolar world of the early 1960's. A more recent film like *Wargames* (1983, 114 minutes, Films, Inc./MGM–UA Home Video) raises the safety issues surrounding computer command and control. Chernobyl and Three Mile Island remind us that it is not only in weapons that nuclear technology poses a potential threat. Global annihilation can now be accomplished chemically and biologically as well as by nuclear weapons, and now many more nations have joined, or are reputed to have joined, the "nuclear club." Discussion that updates the concerns and fears expressed in *Dr. Strangelove* would be very interesting. In addition, discussion can focus on the aspects of the cold war (ideas, technologies, prejudices, personalities, events) that the film reflects and satirizes.

Books and Materials Relating to This Film and Topic

George, Peter. *Red Alert* (Ace, 1958).

Kagan, Norman. *The Cinema of Stanley Kubrick* (Grove, 1972).

Kahn, Herman. *On Thermonuclear War* (Princeton University Press, 1961).

Kissinger, Henry. *Nuclear Weapons and Foreign Policy* (1957).

Whitfield, Stephen J. *The Culture of the Cold War.* (Johns Hopkins, 1990).

Wittner, Lawrence S. *Cold War America* (Praeger, 1974).

Other Media Resources for This Time Period

The Manchurian Candidate (1962, 126 minutes, Swank Motion Pictures/MGM–UA Home Video.) This story about brainwashing, power, and political assassination was withdrawn from circulation by its director, John Frankenheimer, when John F. Kennedy was killed.

On the Beach (1959, 133 minutes, Films, Inc./CBS–Fox Video.) One of the first films to warn of the threat of nuclear holocaust.

The Russians Are Coming! The Russians Are Coming! (1966, 120 minutes, Films, Inc./MGM–UA Home Video) One of the first films to break down the stereotype of the Russians as our mortal enemies.

Unit 10: The Cold War

Dr. Strangelove or: How I Learned to Stop Worrying and Love the Bomb, Columbia Pictures, 1964. Written, produced, and directed by Stanley Kubrick.

Major Character	**Actor**
General Jack D. Ripper	Sterling Hayden
General Buck Turgidson	George C. Scott
President Merkin Muffley	Peter Sellers
Group Captain Lionel Mandrake	Peter Sellers
Dr. Strangelove	Peter Sellers
Major "King" Kong	Slim Pickens
Ambassador de Sadesky	Peter Bull
Colonel Bat Guano	Keenan Wynn

What to Watch For

This controversial film was one of the first in the cold war era to show the military in a critical light and to point out the reality of a possible nuclear incident. Although the Strategic Air Command (SAC) declared its nuclear weapons launch-control system to be "fail-safe"—that is, incapable of being activated by either human insubordination or machine error—Stanley Kubrick, the director of *Dr. Strangelove*, felt otherwise. He wished to illustrate the seriousness of the nuclear threat as well as the paranoia shown by many Americans towards communism.

Kubrick used satire and black comedy to drive home his concerns. Black comedy is comedy that straddles a fine line between horror and humor. It portrays things of such a serious nature that laughter is the only way to break the tension. Some critics wrote that the film was so ludicrous in some ways and in other instances so humorous that it missed its primary objective.

Keep in mind the time in which this film was produced. The Cuban missile crisis (October 1962) was a recent memory and despite the signing of the Nuclear Test Ban Treaty in 1963, the United States military was calling for more missiles, bombers, and bombs to defend against the Soviet Union. The thaw in the cold war had not yet reached the military establishment. And, strategic planners were putting into place a deterrence theory based upon targeting nuclear weapons at one another's cities. If either side started a war, both sides would suffer mutually assured destruction. The resulting theory, which governed both sides' nuclear policy, was called M.A.D.D. for "Mutually Assured Destruction Doctrine." Kubrick's film was a response to this.

The film also proved a great vehicle for one of the most versatile comic actors of the day, Peter Sellers. Much of our current comedy, particularly in programs like "Saturday Night Live," owe much to the genius of Sellers.

Unit 10: The Cold War

Dr. Strangelove or: How I Learned to Stop Worrying and Love the Bomb

Vocabulary

Fail-safe

ICBM (intercontinental ballistic missile)

Megaton

Pentagon

M.A.D.D.

Safeguard

Strategic Air Command

Guano

Turgid

King Kong

Jack the Ripper

Questions Based on the Film

1. Does Major Kong's pep talk to his crew, with its accompanying background music, seem appropriate to the situation in which the crew finds itself? What

   message is Kubrick trying to present in this scene? _____

   _____

   _____

2. What does General Ripper do to secure his base? _____

   _____

   _____

3. Why can't the planes be immediately recalled? _____

   _____

   _____

(continued)

Name _____ Date _____

Dr. Strangelove or: How I Learned to Stop Worrying and Love the Bomb (continued)

4. What is General Turgidson's answer to the "problem" of the attack without presidential authorization? _____

_____

_____

5. According to de Sadesky, why did the Russians build the doomsday machine?

_____

_____

_____

6. What are the characteristics of "real Americans" as General Turgidson, General Ripper, Colonel Guano, and Major Kong might each define them?

_____

_____

_____

7. According to Ripper, what massive Communist conspiracy began in 1946?

_____

_____

_____

8. According to Dr. Strangelove, how should the president determine who should survive in the mine shafts? What long-term benefits to the United States might result from the impending nuclear holocaust? _____

_____

_____

9. Was there some reason beyond a director's desire to get "maximum mileage" from his comedy star that Stanley Kubrick had Peter Sellers play the three particular characters (Group Captain Mandrake, President Muffley, and Dr. Strangelove) that he does in the film? _____

_____

_____

The Civil Rights Movement

Teacher's Guide

The Long Walk Home, New Vision Pictures, 1991. Directed by Richard Pearce, color, 97 minutes. Distributed on videocassette by Live Home Video.

Background of the Film

On December 1, 1955, Rosa Parks was riding home from her job as a seamstress in a downtown Montgomery, Alabama, department store. When the bus driver ordered her to give up her seat to a white passenger as the law required, Mrs. Parks refused. She was arrested and put in jail. The next morning a group of black community leaders including Ralph Abernathy, pastor of the First Baptist Church, called for a one-day boycott of the Montgomery city buses on the day of Rosa Parks's trial. The pastor of the Dexter Avenue Baptist Church, Martin Luther King, Jr., made his church available for meetings. The boycott was supported by such a large proportion of the African American riding public that it was extended.

This film is about two Montgomery families and their experiences during the boycott. The Thompsons are white and affluent; Miriam Thompson is wrapped up in her social round of Junior League bridge parties and hairdresser's appointments. Odessa Cotter is the Thompsons' maid who must walk nine miles from her home with its meager simplicity to the Thompsons' suburban residence.

When this film was released in 1990, it was almost immediately withdrawn because a critic, who said he was in Montgomery during the boycott, questioned the film's premise. It was later discovered that this critic had not been in Montgomery, and the film was rereleased in 1991 with the endorsement of Rosa Parks and many African American leaders.

The film gives a good view of racial attitudes in the segregated South of the 1950's, as well as an interesting glimpse at Miriam Thompson's increasing self-awareness. The Montgomery bus boycott is viewed by many as one of the primary moving events of the civil rights movement, a shining example of the nonviolent protest that culminated 55 weeks later in the city ending the legal segregation of public transportation.

Synopsis of the Plot

The movie takes place in 1955 in Montgomery, Alabama. The opening scene shows African American women entering a bus through the front door, paying their fare, then getting off and entering the bus again through the back door. The story is told from seven-year-old Mary Catherine Thompson's point of view. Odessa Cotter is the Thompson family's maid.

Odessa is told by Miriam Thompson to take Mary Catherine and some friends to the park for a picnic. A policeman throws Odessa out of the whites-only park. Miriam uses her political pull with the police commissioner to force the policeman to apologize to Odessa.

At Odessa's house, her two boys bring notice of a boycott of the buses. Rosa Parks has been arrested for sitting down and refusing to give up her seat to a white person. The next morning the buses go by empty. Miriam decides to pick Odessa up when she calls to say she'll be late to work because she will not ride the bus.

In the evenings, there are meetings to unify and inspire the people as the bus boycott continues. Odessa and her family attend these meetings.

Miriam becomes concerned that Odessa's long walk to and from work is wearing her out. She agrees to pick Odessa up two mornings a week. The police follow Miriam in an effort to harass her. Miriam's husband, Norman, doesn't know that Miriam is taking Odessa to work. When Miriam questions his involvement in a citizen's group to fight the boycott, Norm is furious. When Norm finds out that Miriam is driving Odessa, he forbids her to do it again.

Miriam confronts Norman and tells him not to meddle in the way she runs the household. His reaction is to withdraw to another part of the house and question their entire relationship. Miriam now decides to actively support the bus boycott by volunteering to drive a car-pool from the city to the suburbs.

Norm's brother, Tunker, takes Norm to the car-pool rendezvous where a group of white businessmen have assembled to harass the people waiting for rides. Tunker threatens Miriam, but when he slaps her, Norman goes to her rescue.

Despite the threats and shouts of the white men, the black women stand firm. As they join hands and sing a spiritual, Miriam joins them.

Ideas for Class Discussion

Enough time has now passed since the era of the early civil rights movement for us to begin to analyze and examine it in films such as *Malcolm X* and *Eyes on the Prize*. A fruitful class discussion might be to look at "how far" we have come, what inequalities still need to be addressed, and what methods might properly be used to effectively address these issues. This could be extended to a discussion of gender issues, cultural bias, and the question of sexual orientation.

Books and Materials Relating to This Film and Topic

Cooney, Robert, and Michalowski, Helen, ed. *The Power of the People: Active Nonviolence in the United States* (New Society Publishers, 1987).

King, Martin Luther, Jr. *Stride Toward Freedom: The Montgomery Story* (Harper and Row, 1958).

Other Media Resources for This Time Period

The Court Martial of Jackie Robinson (1990, 93 minutes, Turner Home Entertainment) Directed by Larry Pearce. After experiencing racism on his army base, Robinson refuses to give up his seat in the front of an army bus and is court-martialed for insubordination.

Driving Miss Daisy (1989, 99 minutes, Warner Home Video) Academy Award-winning film about the relationship between an elderly white woman and her black chauffeur.

King (1978, 272 minutes, HBO Video) Directed by Abby Mann. The made-for-television dramatization of the life of civil rights leader Martin Luther King, Jr.

Malcolm X (1992, 201 minutes, Swank Film/Warner Home Video) Directed by Spike Lee. The superb, if occasionally romanticized, account of the spiritual journey of the Black Muslim leader from his troubled childhood until his assassination.

Unit 11: The Civil Rights Movement

The Long Walk Home, New Visions Pictures, 1991. Directed by Richard Pearce.

Major Character	**Actor/Actress**
Odessa Cotter	Whoopi Goldberg
Miriam Thompson	Sissy Spacek
Norman Thompson	Dwight Schultz
Tunker Thompson	Dylan Baker
Cotter	Ving Rhames

What to Watch For

The Montgomery bus boycott of 1955–56 was in a very real sense the beginning of the civil rights movement in the American South. This film portrays the events of the boycott through the eyes of two families, the affluent white family, the Thompsons, and the family of their black maid, Odessa Cotter. The screenwriter of the film, John Cork, grew up in Montgomery, so the behaviors and look of the film are accurate.

Although it may seem shocking today, the attitudes expressed by the whites in the film were not atypical of that time period. It is important to note that despite the existence of the racist white citizen's group, which Norm Thompson joins in the film, there were many whites in Montgomery who did support the boycott. The well-organized car-pool system portrayed did, in fact, exist.

The minister of the church where the blacks go for support is Reverend Martin Luther King, Jr. The Montgomery bus boycott was King's first real success with non-violent protest.

Note the increasing tension between Miriam and her husband. This film also deals with Miriam's growing independence and individualism.

This film was endorsed by Rosa Parks, the woman who "began it all" when on December 1, 1955, she refused to relinquish her bus seat to a white person, which was the law at that time.

Unit 11: The Civil Rights Movement

The Long Walk Home

Vocabulary

Boycott

The Klan

Segregation

Questions Based on The Film

1. Why are the black residents of Montgomery boycotting the city buses?

   _____

   _____

   _____

2. Compare Christmas at the Thompson household with that of the Cotters.

   _____

   _____

   _____

3. What are some of the attitudes expressed by the Thompson relatives about Negroes? _____

   _____

   _____

4. What happens to Selma when she tries to ride the bus to the other side of town?

   _____

   _____

   _____

5. How does Miriam change during the course of the film? _____

   _____

   _____

(continued)

Unit 11: The Civil Rights Movement

The Long Walk Home (continued)

6. What is the reaction of the black citizens when they hear that Dr. King's house
   has been bombed? _____

   _____

   _____

7. Is the boycott successful? Why is this event so significant in the civil rights
   movement? _____

   _____

Unit 12

Life in the Fifties and Sixties

Teacher's Guide

American Graffiti, Universal Pictures, 1972. Directed by George Lucas, color, 110 minutes. Distributed on videocassette by MCA Home Video.

Background of the Film

George Lucas was only 28 years old when he conceived the idea for *American Graffiti* and went on to direct the movie. Students will know Lucas better for the *Star Wars* and *Indiana Jones* movies, but this was his first big hit.

American Graffiti, the first big 1950's nostalgia movie, captures the last moments of American "innocence" before the turbulent 1960's take hold. The time is 1962 and the setting is Modesto, California. Lucas graduated from a high school in Modesto in 1962 and the movie is drawn from his experiences as a teenager. To teenagers in Modesto, "cruising," that is, riding up and down the main street showing off your car to other teenagers, was a way of life; Lucas himself cruised the streets every day from 3:00 in the afternoon until 1:00 A.M. The hub of activity was the drive-in restaurant—Mel's Drive-in in the movie. Lucas based his main characters on people he knew in high school: Steve is the all-American boy, class president, and athlete. Milner is a "greaser" with cigarettes in his rolled-up T-shirt sleeve; Toad is the classic "nerd" and "loser." Curt is the class brain, always quick with a retort. Laurie is head cheerleader, a "good" girl who refuses to have sex with Steve before he goes off to college. Debbie is the "bad" girl who is willing to "put out" for liquor and a nice car.

The actors and actresses playing the roles in *American Graffiti* were relative unknowns when the film was made. Now, of course, they are instantly recognized and many are viewed as major Hollywood stars. Ron Howard was already a television child star, but is now even better known as a director with several hit films, including *Cocoon* and *Parenthood*, to his credit.

The film was budgeted at $700,000, a very low sum even in 1972. It took only 28 nights to shoot. All of the action is compressed into one late summer night and revolves around the parallel adventures and misadventures of the four male friends: Steve Bolander, Curt Henderson, Terry "Toad" Fields, and John Milner. Adults in the film rarely appear; when they do they are pictured as fools, like the high school principal who gives Steve a detention, only to be reminded that he has already graduated, or the policemen whose car is separated from its wheels in the prank played by the Pharaohs gang. The only significant adult in this world populated by teenagers is Wolfman Jack, a real-life legendary figure from the late 1950's. He became famous as a disc jockey on a Mexican radio station that could be heard from coast to coast. The Wolfman becomes a Wizard of Oz-like character, part of the teen's world of fantasy. But in reality, as Curt finds out, he is really a great pretender. Wolfman and his music are a connecting thread throughout the film.

American Graffiti went on to make Universal Studios a profit of $350 million. It started a nostalgia craze that resulted in television shows like "Happy Days" and "Laverne and Shirley." Baby boomers, disillusioned by the strife-torn America of the 1960's, nostalgically relived their 1950's youth as a time when there was a sense of community in shared values, language, humor, and music. As Dale Pollock, author of *Skywalking, The Life and Films of George Lucas*, writes: "The secret of the success of *Graffiti* is that it works on two levels, as a 'kids-goofing-off movie,' and as an anthropological statement about American culture and mores" (p. 29, Harmony Books, 1983).

Synopsis of the Plot

The time is 1962; the place, Modesto, a town in California. All the action takes place during a single night in late summer between sunset and dawn.

The opening scene is at Mel's Drive-in, the local hamburger joint and hangout for teenagers. Two friends, Steve and Curt, are leaving town the next morning to go east to college. Steve leaves his car with another friend, Terry (Toad), who immediately decides to take up the favorite recreation of teenagers, cruising the main streets. Their other friend, John Milner, is a car mechanic, who is noted as being the top drag racer in town and has never been beaten. The plot switches back and forth among these four friends and what happens to them on this night.

Steve and his girlfriend Laurie go to a school dance. Laurie doesn't want Steve to leave the next day and they fight over their relationship. Milner ends up with a twelve-year-old named Carol in his car, much to his disgust. He is also being pursued by Bob Falfa, who wants to race him. Curt is searching for a blonde in a white T-Bird who mouthed the words "I love you" and mysteriously disappeared. He finds himself coerced into joining members of the Pharaohs gang for part of the evening and even becomes an unwilling party to their pranks and lawbreaking. Toad picks up a girl, Debbie, and while they are off drinking and necking, the car is stolen.

Milner is finally able to take Carol home and helps Toad recover Steve's car. Laurie and Steve have split up and Laurie is picked up by Bob Falfa. Curt finally leaves the company of the Pharaohs and drives to the outskirts of town in search of the legendary Wolfman. He meets instead a fairly ordinary man who is eating popsicles and playing records. As the sun comes up, Milner and Falfa race and Falfa's car crashes. He and Laurie escape just before the car bursts into flames. Laurie and Steve are reconciled and Curt receives a phone call from the mysterious blonde.

Curt ultimately leaves to go to college, but Steve decides to stay. As Curt's plane takes off, the last thing he sees is a white T-Bird going down the road. As a postscript, Lucas tells what happens to each of the four friends, while a Beach Boys song heralds a new type of music unlike the traditional rock 'n' roll of the 1950's.

Ideas for Class Discussion

American Graffiti is a great film to discuss with teenagers since it is about high school students. What changes have occurred in teenagers' lives in the past thirty years? How have their social customs, such as dating or entertainment, changed? In 1962, young people were facing the beginning of the Vietnam era. What uncertainties do they face today?

Books and Materials Relating to This Film and Topic

Doherty, Thomas. *Teenagers and Teenpics: The Juvenilization of American Movies in the 1950's* (Unwin Hyman, 1988).

Pollock, Dale. *Skywalking: The Life and Films of George Lucas* (Harmony Books, 1983).

Other Media Resources for This Time Period

Back to the Future (1985, 116 minutes, Swank Motion Pictures/MCA Home Video) Time travel movie of the 1950's.

Four Friends (1981, 115 minutes, Warner Home Video) Looks at the youth revolution of the 1960's.

The Invasion of the Body Snatchers (1956, 80 minutes, Films, Inc./Republic Pictures Home Video) Sometimes regarded as a classic, this film deals with the issues of coercion, conformity, and the struggle against them during the 1950's. This version is preferred over the big-budget remake, which is also available on video.

The Last Picture Show (1971, 118 minutes, Films, Inc.) A look back at small-town America in the 1950's. A sequel, called *Texasville* (1990, 126 minutes, Nelson Entertainment) explores the kinds of adult lives the major characters led.

Peggy Sue Got Married (1986, 104 minutes, Films, Inc./CBS–Fox Video) Time-travel movie that takes us back to the 1950's.

Unit 12: Life in the Fifties and Sixties

American Graffiti, Universal Pictures, 1972. Directed by George Lucas.

Major Character	**Actor/Actress**
Curt Henderson	Richard Dreyfuss
Steve Bolander	Ron Howard
John Milner	Paul LeMat
Terry "Toad" Fields	Charlie Martin Smith
Laurie	Cindy Williams
Debbie	Candy Clark
Carol	Mackenzie Phillips
Disc Jockey	Wolfman Jack
Bob Falfa	Harrison Ford
Girl in Car	Suzanne Somers

What to Watch For

This film was the first big hit for director George Lucas of *Star Wars* and *Indiana Jones* movie fame. It also was the first film to capitalize on a growing sense of nostalgia for the "good old days" of the 1950's.

The action takes place in one single summer night in Modesto, California, in 1962. It tells of the adventures of four friends from high school, who have graduated and now must find their niche in the larger world.

This movie was very low budget and took only 28 days to shoot. The actors and actresses were mostly unknowns, and this movie proved to be their ticket to fame.

Note the role of music in this movie. Wolfman Jack was a popular disc jockey of the late 1950's, a time in which music, particularly rock 'n' roll, separated the generations.

Critics believe that this movie portrays the last moment of American innocence before we became engulfed in the Vietnam War and the domestic turbulence of the 1960's. The world of the teenagers, isolated from the outside, was one of cars, hamburger joints, and music. Even adults do not intrude very often in this movie. "Baby Boomers" (those born immediately after World War II ended) loved *American Graffiti*. It made a tremendous profit for Universal Studios and a millionaire of George Lucas. Many other films and TV shows set in the 1950's (*Back to the Future*, "Happy Days," "Laverne and Shirley") owe their inspiration to this movie and to the underlying desire to look back fondly at a time when life seemed much simpler.

Unit 12: Life in the Fifties and Sixties

American Graffiti

Vocabulary

It seems that every period in history has a popular vocabulary uniquely its own. While viewing this film, see if you can make a list of slang expressions used by the teenagers, such as "Holstein" for a police patrol car, and "J.D." for a juvenile delinquent. How do these compare with expressions used by teenagers today?

Questions Based on the Film

1. How are adults portrayed in the film? _____

   _____

   _____

2. Compare the amusements and diversions of teenagers in the early 1960's with those of teenagers today. Do you think that these were peculiar to California culture? _____

   _____

   _____

3. Compare the high school hop in the film with dances held today. _____

   _____

   _____

4. We think of youth gangs as a new phenomenon. What were gangs like in the time that this movie portrays? How are they different today? _____

   _____

   _____

5. Are there still kids like Steve, Curt, Toad, and Milner today? _____

   _____

   _____

6. What happens to the four friends ultimately? Was this foreshadowed in any way? _____

   _____

   _____

The Vietnam War

A Teacher's Guide to Feature Films and Documentary Sources

The Vietnam War has a plethora of media resources, but many are inappropriate for school use. This unit will present an annotated list of feature films that you may wish to view for your own education, some feature films that may be used in class, and documentaries relating to the Vietnam experience.

N/A means that a film is not currently available for educational distribution on film or video. An asterisk (*) indicates that a film is appropriate for classroom use.

Feature Films on Vietnam

Saigon (1948, 94 minutes, Paramount Pictures/Swank Motion Pictures) The first post-World War II American film on Vietnam, it is a formula piece in which Saigon could be any mysterious locale.

China Gate (1957, 120 minutes, Globe Enterprises Productions/Ivy Classics Video) A "B"-Movie-Director Samuel Fuller film about American mercenaries in the French Foreign Legion during the French war in Indochina. Nat King Cole plays one of the soldiers, Lee Van Cleef plays the Viet Minh general, and Angie Dickinson is introduced to the public in this film. She plays a half-caste Vietnamese woman. The film makes a point about racial tolerance at the end.

The Quiet American (1958, 120 minutes, United Artists/Films, Inc.) Note that the film turns Graham Greene's story of murderous naiveté on its head to make a cold war point.

Feature Films About Our Involvement in Vietnam and the Vietnam Era

A Yank in Vietnam (1964, 80 minutes, Allied Artists), N/A. First combat film about Americans in Vietnam, and one of the few films actually shot in Vietnam. The plot revolves around the capture of a U.S. Army officer and a Vietnamese doctor by the Viet Cong.

*The Green Berets (1968, 141 minutes, Warner Brothers/Swank Video) Typical John Wayne good guy/bad guy film with Wayne portraying a Special Forces commander. Exemplifies the pro-war attitude felt by many.

Alice's Restaurant (1969, 111 minutes, MGM/United Artists) Taken from Arlo Guthrie's song, it chronicles his problems with the local police and his draft board.

Getting Straight (1970, 124 minutes, Columbia Pictures/Ivy Classics Video) Film that deals with the antiwar movement on U.S. campuses, though it somewhat understates its intellectual commitment, substituting for it hormonal drives and middle-class draft avoidance.

Billy Jack (1971, 112 minutes, Warner Brothers) One of several films about a renegade veteran who fights against bigotry and injustice on the home front. Rated PG. It is in some ways a precursor to the first *Rambo* film that is set in the Pacific Northwest.

Summertree (1971, 88 minutes, Columbia Pictures/Budget Films) A coming-of-age film with the Vietnam War as the backdrop.

*Trial of the Catonsville Nine (1972, 85 minutes, Melville Productions/Zenger Video) Dramatizes the trial of two Catholic priests, Daniel and Philip Berrigan, and seven others for antiwar and antidraft activities.

Rolling Thunder (1977, 99 minutes, American International Pictures/Swank Motion Pictures) A POW seeks revenge when thugs kill his wife and son his revenge really taking on a wider role in seeking retribution for his Vietnam experiences.

The Boys In Company C (1978, 126 minutes Columbia Pictures/Swank Motion Pictures) A film that follows recruits from boot camp to combat in Vietnam. It is a transitional film in that, although the soldiers recognize the futility and corruption of the war, they continue fighting it for the sake of their unit's pride.

Coming Home (1978, 126 minutes, United Artists/Films, Inc.) Film about a love triangle between a paraplegic Vietnam veteran, a marine officer, and his wife.

The Deer Hunter (1978, 183 minutes, Universal/Swank Motion Pictures/MCA Home Video) The sprawling story of three steelworkers from Pittsburgh who join the Army and are captured by the Viet Cong. The Russian roulette episodes, which are unsubstantiated by the histories of the war, present the film's most riveting and controversial metaphors.

Who'll Stop the Rain (1978, 126 minutes, United Artists/Films, Inc.) Based on Robert Stone's novel *Dog Soldiers* about how the lunacy of the war fed the domestic drug market and corrupted the institutions and relationships it was being fought to defend.

Apocalypse Now (1979, 150 minutes, United Artists/Films, Inc.) Directed by Francis Ford Coppola and loosely based on Joseph Conrad's *Heart of Darkness* and Sir James Frazier's *The Golden Bough*, both written at the turn of the century. This film takes the Vietnam War into the realm of epic mythology and has been written about and interpreted more than any other film about Vietnam. Rated R.

Hair (1979, 121 minutes, United Artists/MGM–UA Video) Expatriate Czech director Milos Foreman's incisive adaptation of the late-sixties counterculture musical that sets its blackout numbers into a narrative line about a group of hippies, led by Treat Williams, who try to convince army recruit John Savage not to go to Vietnam. It serves as a kind of summary statement about the attitudes of the American public toward the war.

*Friendly Fire (1979, 145 minutes, ABC-TV/Zenger Video) The true story of two parents who are radicalized by the U.S. government's self-serving indifference to the death of their son in Vietnam.

*A Rumor of War (1980, 200 minutes, United Artists/MGM–United Artists Video) A made-for-TV movie based on Philip Caputo's novel, it follows a group of soldiers caught up in the horror and moral ambiguities of the war in Vietnam.

The Big Chill (1983, 105 minutes, Columbia Pictures/Films, Inc.) A group of yuppie friends reminisce about college in the sixties and how their lives have changed. Rated R.

The Killing Fields (1984, 141 minutes, Swank Motion Pictures/Warner Home Video) A true story about the destruction of Cambodia in the wake of the Vietnam War, told from the point of view of *New York Times* correspondent Sidney Schonberg and his Cambodian photographer/interpreter Dith Pran, whom he is forced to leave behind when the country falls to the Khmer Rouge.

Alamo Bay (1985, 85 minutes, Tri-Star Pictures/RCA–Columbia Pictures Home Video, Films, Inc.) This film tells the story of the clash between Vietnamese refugees and American workers whose jobs were threatened in a Texas fishing port. Rated R.

Platoon (1986, 120 minutes, Hemdale Pictures/Swank Motion Pictures/Vestron Video) Academy Award-winning film about the war in the jungles of Vietnam. Many Vietnam veterans regard the atmosphere created by Vietnam veteran Oliver Stone in this film as the most accurate re-creation yet of how the war actually felt, despite its monochromatic portrait of good and evil embodied in its two sergeant protagonists. Rated R.

Full Metal Jacket (1987, 118 minutes, Warner Brothers/Swank Motion Pictures/Warner Home Video) Stanley Kubrick's film about the training and combat action of soldiers in Hue during the Tet offensive. Rated R.

Gardens of Stone (1987, 112 minutes, Tri-Star Pictures/Films, Inc./CBS–Fox Home Video) Francis Ford Coppola's film about the moral conflict felt by the soldiers of the Old Guard stationed at Fort Meyer, Virginia, in 1968, who provide the burial detachment at Arlington Cemetery on the home front during the war.

Good Morning Vietnam (1987, 120 minutes, Buena Vista/Films, Inc./Touchstone Home Video) Starring Robin Williams, story of an Armed Forces radio DJ who angers his superiors in Saigon by his unorthodox actions. It is very loosely based on the experiences of Adrian Cronauer. Rated R.

Hamburger Hill (1987, 110 minutes, Paramount Pictures/Films, Inc./Vestron Video) Recreates the May 1969 ten-day assault on a heavily fortified Viet Cong position on Dong Ap Bia, a mountain in the A Shau Valley. Heavily covered by the media including *Life* magazine, which published the photographs of 241 soldiers killed in the first seven days of the battle, Hamburger Hill was the last of the attrition battles as President Nixon's Vietnamization policy replaced the "meat-grinder" tactics of U.S. combat operations. At the end of the battle, the North Vietnamese retreated across the border into Laos and the Americans abandoned the mountain. Rated R.

The Iron Triangle (1988, 194 minutes, IVE) Shows the war through an American POW's growing understanding of his adversary. Rated R.

Documentaries About the Vietnam Era (which can be used in classes)

Why Vietnam? (1965, 32 minutes, U.S. Department of Defense/Zenger Video) Presents official U.S. government rationale used to justify air involvement in Vietnam.

The Anderson Platoon (1967, 65 minutes, Films, Inc.) This early French documentary follows a combat platoon during six weeks in the central highlands of Vietnam.

In the Year of the Pig (1969, 103 minutes, New Yorker Films) Contains a history of French and American involvement in Vietnam.

Hearts and Minds (1974, 112 minutes, Warner Brothers/Columbia Pictures) Complex documentary that deals as much with American society as it does with the Vietnam War.

The War at Home (1979, 100 minutes, Wisconsin Educational Television Network/Zenger Video) Focuses on radical students at the University of Wisconsin and the antiwar movement in the United States.

Vietnam: The Ten Thousand Day War (1980, 49 minutes per episode, Nelson Entertainment) Thirteen episodes.

Vietnam—Chronicle of a War (1981, 89 minutes, CBS News/Zenger Video) Uses the CBS archives to document the history of the Vietnam War and traces our involvement year by year.

Vietnam: A Television History (1983, 60 minutes per episode, PBS/Zenger Video/Films, Inc.) Thirteen episodes chronicle the Vietnam War; widely acclaimed, but not without its critics.

The Bloods of 'Nam (1986, 58 minutes, PBS Video) and *Remembering My Lai* (1989, 58 minutes, PBS Video) are two programs from the Public Broadcasting Service's *Frontline* series.

Dear America: Letter Home from Vietnam (1987, 84 minutes, HBO Films/Zenger Video) Documentary produced for cable television which shows the Vietnam experiences through the letters of American soldiers.

After 'Nam: CNN Special Report (1988, 30 minutes, Cable News Network/Zenger Video) Investigative report that looks at the effects of the Vietnam War.

Television's Vietnam, Part 1 and Part 2 (1984, 116 minutes, Accuracy In Media/Facets Video) Basically a conservative response to the PBS series *Vietnam, A Television History,* it uses many of the same techniques to sway audience opinion that it accuses the PBS series of using.

Books Relating to Media on the Vietnam Era

Adair, Gilbert. *Vietnam on Film* (Proteus Books, 1981).

Auster, Albert, and Quart, Leonard. *How the War Was Remembered: Hollywood and Vietnam* (Praeger, 1988).

Christensen, Terry. *Reel Politics: American Political Movies from Birth of a Nation to Platoon* (Basil Blackwell, 1987).

Dittmar, Linda, and Michaud, Gene, ed. *From Hanoi to Hollywood: The Vietnam War in American Film* (Rutgers University Press, 1990).

Hellman, John. *American Myth and the Legacy of Vietnam* (Columbia University Press, 1986).

Klein, Michael, and Wiesner, Peter. "A Filmography of Oppositional Politics and Culture in the Vietnam Era, 1963–1974." *Historical Journal of Film, Radio and Television,* Vol. 11, No. 1, 1991, pp. 59–72.

Rollins, Peter C. *Hollywood as Historian* (University of Kentucky Press, 1983).

Rowe, John Carlos, and Berg, Rick. *The Vietnam War and American Culture* (Columbia University Press, 1991).

Walsh, Jeffrey, and Aulich, James, ed. *Vietnam Images: War and Representation* (St. Martin's Press, 1989).

Unit 14

The End of the Twentieth Century

Teacher's Guide

Nightbreaker, Symphony Pictures Corporation, 1988. Directed by Peter Markle, color, 99 minutes. Distributed on videocassette by Turner Home Entertainment and Movies Unlimited.

Background of the Film

Although the names are fictionalized, this movie provides a look back at a shocking episode in our nation's history: the use of U.S. soldiers as virtual guinea pigs at atomic test sites. During the 1950's, military planners considered nuclear weapons to be usable in close infantry support situations. Members of the 82nd Airborne, led by Corporal Russell Jack Dann (thinly disguised as Sergeant Jack Russell in the film), were brought onto the Nevada test site in 1957 for a series of experiments called Shot Smoky. In 1951 the Army had formed a Human Resources Research Office (HUMRRO) to look at the psychological effects of atomic warfare. At Shot Smoky, HUMRRO psychologists wanted to know if soldiers who had witnessed an atomic detonation would be too shocked or panicked to complete their combat tasks. Secondly, they wanted to know if the soldiers' fear of radiation would impair their ability to perform in battle. The idea for the study, as explained in *Nightbreaker,* came from the Battle of Petersburg during the Civil War. Union troops had tunneled under the Confederate lines and loaded the tunnel with explosives. After the blast, the Union troops failed to act and just stood and gawked at the hole. HUMRRO wanted to find out if this would happen after an atomic explosion. Questionnaires were used to discover the soldiers' attitudes and knowledge about atomic bombs. This had all been tried before at test sites in Nevada, so there is a question as to why yet another group of soldiers was exposed to atomic testing.

As shown in the film, pigs were used as test animals. To conduct an experiment called Test Priscilla, army uniforms were made for the pigs in order to test radiation on skin dressed in army clothes.

Some soldiers were given radiation film badges to wear to measure the dosage of radiation that they were receiving; however, these had not been proven to be accurate. It also appears that the U.S. Army changed the safe distance and radiation limit from test to test and the soldiers were not told what exposure they were receiving. In attempting to conduct follow-up studies of these "atomic soldiers," many private researchers found that their army medical records and/or all records of their exposure to radiation had disappeared. The government has not acknowledged any correlation between illnesses suffered by the soldiers and their exposure to radiation.

Synopsis of the Plot

The plot of this film moves from the present (1988) back to 1956, intercutting between the experiences of Dr. Alexander Brown in both time periods.

Dr. Brown is in Las Vegas, Nevada, to receive an award as Neurologist of the Year. He is visited in his hotel room by a group of veterans and a man in a wheelchair. They want Brown to testify that he was part of an experiment, Project Nightbreaker, which sent soldiers close to an atomic detonation. Brown refuses.

The movie then flashes back to 1956, when Brown arrived in the Nevada desert to work with Dr. Roscoe Cummings. The place swarms with media people and spectators who applaud when the atomic bomb is detonated. Brown and Cummings are part of a project to interview soldiers about their attitudes toward nuclear warfare. The 76th Airborne is the group with whom Brown works. The supposed purpose of the project is to see if troops can witness an atomic blast and then take military advantage of it by seizing and securing objectives immediately after the blast.

Alex meets Sally Mathews, who is also working at the test site. Near the blast site, Sally and Alex set up a model house typical of the time period with dummies as inhabitants. At dawn, the soldiers are sent close to the blast site and are put in trenches. The debris from the explosion washes over the platoon and they are told to march to "ground zero," the actual point of detonation. The house and dummies are shown to be obliterated.

Back at camp, the soldiers and equipment are measured for radiation and then washed. Dr. Hatch, Sally's boss, and Colonel Devereau, who is in charge of the experiments, argue over the use of soldiers at a site with so much radiation. Sally tells Alex that the troops are being used as guinea pigs. Alex begins to question what he is doing. He goes into the files and finds out that his study has been done before and thus is being unnecessarily replicated.

The scene switches back to the present. A reporter keeps trying to pry into Brown's past. Brown's wife questions him about his experiences at the site. She is upset because she has always thought that their inability to have children was her fault.

Back at the test site in 1956, the soldiers are wrestling with test animals to get them into "radiation-proof" coverings. Later, the soldiers watch a film of the blast destroying the model house. By mistake, they are also shown the test animals being maimed by the blast and the radiation.

The soldiers prepare to go to a party at Sally's house, but when they arrive she refuses to let them in. She has learned that fallout from the last test blast has contaminated them.

Devereau warns Alex against fraternizing with the test subjects. Alex confronts him with changing the safe dosage level and lying to the soldiers.

Back in the present, Brown returns to the test site and remembers a time when he and the soldiers were moved to a point practically at ground zero. He remembers how the soldiers received the full force of the blast. At the dinner party where Brown has accepted his award, the veterans move into the room. Brown refuses to read his prepared remarks and decides to speak about his experiences at ground zero.

The movie ends with a final flashback of young Dr. Brown leaving the test site. Actual footage is then shown of soldiers at the site and the following words appear: "Between 1945 and 1962 over 235,000 servicemen and women were involved in above-ground atomic tests."

Ideas for Class Discussion

This film could lead to a class discussion about experimentation and the use of humans as guinea pigs. Is this ever justified? Should the rights of the individual ever be violated for the common good of the nation as a whole? And, of course, this film brings up the entire issue of nuclear safety, from weaponry to the use of nuclear energy. Today, soldiers from the Gulf War are complaining of various ills that they believe were caused by exposure to radioactive materials used in weapons.

Books and Materials Relating to This Film and Topic

Boyer, Paul. *By the Bomb's Early Light: American Thought and Culture at the Dawn of the Atomic Age* (Pantheon, 1985).

Browne, Corinne, and Munroe, Robert. *Time Bomb: Understanding the Threat of Nuclear Power* (William Morrow and Company, Inc., 1981).

Medvedev, Zhoris. *Nuclear Disaster in the Urals* (Random House, 1980).

Rafferty, Kevin, Loader, Jane, and Rafferty, Pierce. *The Atomic Café* (Bantam, 1982).

Rosenberg, Howard L. *Atomic Soldiers: American Victims of Nuclear Experiments* (Beacon Press, 1980).

Other Media Resources for This Time Period

Atomic Café (1982, 88 minutes, New Yorker Films/Thorn-EMI Video) A documentary about the fifteen-year-long effort by the U.S. government to convince the public that nuclear war presented an acceptable level of risk.

The China Syndrome (1979, 123 minutes, Films, Inc./RCA–Columbia Pictures Home Video) A film about potentially unsafe conditions in a civilian nuclear power plant.

Coma (1978, 113 minutes, Films, Inc./MGM–UA Home Video) M.D.-turned-writer and director Michael Crichton's mystery about the intersection of biotechnology and amoral capitalism.

Desert Bloom (1986, 106 minutes, Films, Inc./RCA–Columbia Pictures Home Video) A story about the strains on a Nevada family that are aggravated by the atomic tests nearby.

Rage (1972, 104 minutes, Modern Sound Pictures/Warner Home Video) George C. Scott's directoral debut in a film in which he stars as a sheep rancher whose son is exposed to chemical-weapons testing in the military. After the young man's death, his father sets out to identify those responsible.

Silkwood (1983, 131 minutes, Films, Inc./Nelson Entertainment) A film biography of the plutonium plant worker and union activist who was mysteriously killed in a car crash while en route to testify against the unsafe Kerr-McGee company that employed her.

Played out into the future, these contemporary threats (and others) have caused filmmakers to imagine a range of alternative futures, some of which are:

Mad Max Beyond Thunderdome (1985, 109 minutes, Swank Motion Pictures/Warner Home Video) The only one of the *Mad Max* films with a PG-13 rating. Sets its future in a post-energy-crisis environment.

Soylent Green (1973, 97 minutes, Films, Inc./MGM–UA Home Video) Creates a future of overpopulation and food shortage.

Testament (1983, 90 minutes, Films, Inc./Paramount Home Video) and *Planet of the Apes* (1968, 112 minutes, Films, Inc./CBS–Fox Video) are examples of, respectively, near and distant postnuclear holocaust futures.

Unit 14: The End of the Twentieth Century

Nightbreaker, Symphony Pictures, 1988. Directed by Peter Markle.

Major Character	Actor/Actress
Alexander Brown (past)	Emilio Estevez
Alexander Brown (present)	Martin Sheen
Sally Mathews	Lea Thompson
Sergeant Jack Russell	Joe Pantoliano
Paula Brown	Melinda Dillon
Dr. Roscoe Cummings	Paul Eiding
Colonel William Deverau	Nicholas Pryor
Dr. Hatch	Michael Laskin

What to Watch For

This little-known film takes a look at a shocking episode in our nation's history: the use by the military of soldiers as guinea pigs at atomic test sites. The names are fictionalized, but the story is based on fact. Members of the 82nd Airborne (76th Airborne in the film), led by Corporal Russell Jack Dann (Sergeant Jack Russell in the film) were brought to Nevada in 1957 to participate in a series of experiments called Shot Smoky.

Note the carnival atmosphere of the spectator viewing area at the test site. It was considered a great privilege to be able to view an atomic bomb detonation. In nearby Las Vegas, advertisements based on atomic testing urged buyers to take advantage of "atomic bomb drops on high prices." The whole idea of having a test site nearby was looked upon as a money-maker, a tourist draw. How does this relate to today's concerns about atomic power and to how people feel about having a nuclear power plant nearby?

Note the questions asked the soldiers by Dr. Brown as part of the experiment and the soldiers' naiveté about the atomic bomb and radiation. Also note the lecture that the soldiers are given about this experiment and how they will be perfectly safe. The radiation or film badge that is talked about was supposed to be worn by all soldiers to measure radiation; in reality, however, not all received a badge and the records of radiation dosage for those who wore badges have been either lost or destroyed. It is known that the army kept raising the safe dosage limit during the course of the experiments. The army has not acknowledged any correlation between health problems suffered by soldiers and their participation in exercises at the atomic test sites.

Unit 14: The End of the Twentieth Century

Nightbreaker

Vocabulary

Radiation
Fallout
Geiger counter
Ground zero
AEC (Atomic Energy Commission)

Questions Based on the Film

1. What is the atmosphere at the test site when the young Dr. Brown first arrives?

    _____

    _____

    _____

2. What are Sally's feelings about the bomb explosion and the spectators' reactions?

    _____

    _____

    _____

3. What is the purpose of Project Nightbreaker? _____

    _____

    _____

4. When the soldiers are watching the film of the blast, how and why does their

    attitude change? _____

    _____

    _____

5. What do Dr. Hatch and Colonel Deverau argue about? _____

    _____

    _____

6. Why does Alex begin to change his mind about the necessity of the project?

    _____

    _____

    _____

Teaching Media Literacy Through Film: The OK Corral Gunfight—A Case Study

Teacher's Guide

Films on historical subjects that are used in classes to bring a period, person, or event to life are rarely completely faithful to the facts they are re-creating. Through reading, lecture, or discussion, teachers attempt to compensate for these inaccuracies, often relating them to the concerns or biases contemporary with the film's production with which its producers were trying to capture audience attention. But setting mere words against the multisensory immersion of a well-crafted film often leaves the teacher feeling less involved in teaching skills of visual literacy and interpretive sophistication than in confirming old misinformation.

To help students understand that there indeed is an interpretive structure embedded within each narrative and that current concerns do influence presentations of the past, "fire should be fought with fire." Time permitting, it is possible to teach these lessons in precisely this way. For producers—especially Hollywood producers—are loath to let a good story (especially a historical one, concerning familiar public figures) get away. As a result, there are a number of stories from U.S. history that have been filmed over and over again for an American public at different points in their development (enduring the Depression, fighting the antifascist crusade, confronting the cold war, facing the New Frontier, or slogging through the Vietnam quagmire) by filmmakers with their own prejudices and concerns. Carefully selecting groupings of such films, showing them when teaching about the periods in which they were produced, and comparing their interpretations of the historical event they are presenting with both accepted historical canon, and with one another, may result in students developing improved visual literacy skills, more sophisticated interpretive understanding, and a clearer recognition of how past and present are subtly interrelated.

A number of U.S. history topics lend themselves to this pedagogical technique. They include the Civil War, the expansion of the country at the expense of its native inhabitants, race relations, the nature and impact of immigration, the labor wars, the Depression, World War II and the decision to drop the atom bomb, the civil rights movement, and the Vietnam War. The films we have chosen to illustrate this technique are about an episode in the "civilizing" of the West that has entered the realm of mythology—the confrontation between the Earps and the Clantons at Tombstone, Arizona's OK Corral in 1881. At least eight theatrical films[*] have retold the story, beginning with *Law and Order* in 1932; yet none is very accurate when compared with what historians say actually happened there.

The three most famous renditions of the event were produced at important points in the United States' post-World War II history: John Ford's *My Darling Clementine* (1946) was made as Americans were readjusting their sights from beating the Axis to the challenges of reconversion at home and the "menace," both at home and abroad, of communism; John Sturges's *Gunfight at the OK Corral* (1957) was produced at the midpoint of the Eisenhower period of domestic conformity, organized crime revelations, juvenile delinquency, and cold war confrontation in which the United States saw itself as the world's moral arbiter and global policeman; Pete Hamill's *Doc* (1971) appeared as Nixon's "positive polarization" was frustrating the civil rights movement and creating a society at war with itself at home, while the continuing Vietnam War fragmented the country. A careful investigation of each of the three films, paying close attention to not only the moral qualities of the main protagonists and the way in which the gunfight itself is characterized, but also the visualization of the towns in which the action takes place and their inhabitants, teachers can help students to understand the values and biases of the period in which each film was made. And when the films are compared to one another, issues of visual literacy (the ways in which sound, picture, and plot are manipulated to structure the audience's sympathy and understanding), historical interpretation, and the interaction of past and present (the uses the present makes of the past) appear in high contrast. Fire is indeed fought with fire.

Because of the complexity of this unit, more extensive background and plot synopsis material is being provided. Both because of time constraints and because the film *Doc* is emblematic of the rebellion against traditional values that characterized the 1960's, not only in its depictions of political authority, law enforcement, and

---

[*] In addition there has appeared a five-part version of the story as the concluding episodes of the long-running television series, "The Life and Legend of Wyatt Earp" (ABC Television, 1958–1961), which the audience was assured was faithfully re-created from the pages of the *Tombstone Epitaph* (though the audience was not told that the *Epitaph*—one of two Tombstone newspapers—was the mouthpiece of the Republican supporters of the Earp gang). David Wolper produced a documentary about the incident in his *Appointment With Destiny* series, called "Showdown at OK Corral" (1972). The town of Tombstone itself—"the town too tough to die"—daily re-creates the gunfight (with the Earps as its clear heroes) to keep its tourist lifeblood flowing.

able for high school use. The project will work just as well with the two earlier films, but if the sixties are to be included, the extensive plot summary included here will give students what they need to understand the film and to make the comparisons. From an operational standpoint each film should be shown separately and students should be encouraged to carefully fill out the reproducible pages for it, not only to answer questions in discussion about that particular film, but as a memory aid to assist them in making the comparisons and reaching the conclusions about their similarities and differences later on.

Background of the Films

In 1878 silver was discovered in the San Pedro Valley in southeastern Arizona. Within a year, territory that had previously been inhabited by Apaches and a few scrub ranchers, who eked out a living running cattle (their own and others') back and forth across the Mexican border, was overrun with miners hoping to make their fortunes and with others hoping to make their livings by serving the miners' needs. By 1880 the tent settlement of Tombstone that had been set up to service the miners was being gradually displaced by a permanent grid town. By the year's end, there were over three thousand claims and the extracting mills were producing a half million dollars worth of bullion per month. A reservoir and conduit brought water into the town, a church was being built, and all manner of amenities were available. In addition to the hundred or so liquor sellers, restaurants, innumerable brothels, and gambling halls, Tombstone in 1881 had two banks, a fifty-room hotel, four theaters, four shoe stores, three clothing stores, two hardware stores, two blacksmiths, three livery stables, four lumberyards, and four meat markets. There were two newspapers, a photography studio, eight lawyers, two dentists, two druggists, and five physicians. The town also had a large Chinese section, referred to as "Hop Town," and a smaller segregated Mexican quarter. Chinese and Mexicans performed many of the menial and household chores of the town. Though Tombstone failed to attract the railroad, it would soon come to within twenty miles, making the town and its surrounding diggings both accessible and attractive.

Boomtowns like Tombstone were inherently unstable. The Apaches, embittered by the conditions of their captivity on the nearby San Carlos Reservation, were still a threat to settlers in that part of Arizona. The ranchers who controlled Cochise County found their power challenged by the miners and their town-based suppliers. In the resulting power struggle, the townsmen sought support from the Republican territorial administration, while the ranchers—who were called "cowboys" or "The County Ring"—identified themselves as Democrats. The townsmen sought law and order to protect and stabilize their prosperity and property, while the cowboys wanted to retain the older, more tolerant live-and-let-live system that had existed before the boom. The ready-made market for cattle, which the silver strike and the nearby San Carlos Indian reservation with its military overseers promised, drew the cowboys closer to Tombstone. By the end of 1877, N.H. "Old Man" Clanton and his sons Ike, Phin, Peter, and Billy had established a ranch fourteen miles southwest of Tombstone. Newcomers Frank and Tom McLowery would establish themselves on a neighboring ranch. Gunman, killer, and sometime-lawman Johnny Ringo also drifted into the San Pedro Valley to join in the cross-border rustling.

It was into this volatile environment that the Earp brothers came between 1879 and 1881 with their common-law wives, children, and assorted associates. They would make their way as gamblers, saloon keepers, express guards, sometime-lawmen, and when need or profit demanded it, they were not averse to an occasional criminal act. James, the eldest, his brother Virgil, who worked most regularly as a lawman, and Wyatt, who had the most checkered career and the biggest reputation, came first. Morgan and Warren, the youngest, followed and finally Wyatt's friend, the tubercular dentist-turned-gambler, John Henry "Doc" Holliday arrived with his volatile Hungarian-born mistress, "Big Nose" Katie Elder (or Fisher).

What happened in Tombstone in 1880 and 1881 remains a matter of controversy. The Earps became involved, mostly unsuccessfully, in Republican town politics. In 1881 Wyatt lost the Cochise County deputy sheriff's job to Democrat John Behan, with whom he was competing for the affection of a young actress named Josie (Sadie) Marcus, but got himself appointed deputy territorial marshal for southern Arizona by the Republican territorial authorities. In June 1881 Virgil was appointed to the job of town marshal and deputized his brothers. In March of that year three men robbed a stagecoach of about $8,260 and killed its driver and a passenger. Doc Holliday (and by implication the Earps as well) were suspected in the affair. In a fit of anger, Katie Elder filed a deposition accusing Doc, and the Earps were seen carrying suspiciously heavy luggage on their frequent trips to visit their parents in California. The Earp supporters accused members of the cowboy faction of robbing the stage and of protecting the guilty. At one point Wyatt tried to enlist Ike Clanton's assistance in either bringing them to justice or silencing them permanently (depending on who is believed).

In the summer of 1881, Mexican forces ambushed and killed the patriarch of the Clanton family while he was on a cattle raid across the border. Shortly thereafter, yet another stagecoach was robbed. Charges flew back and forth between the Earp faction and the cowboy faction over who was responsible, and all sorts of minor insults and rumors fueled the animosity. The famous gunfight took place on October 26, 1881, after several days of name-calling and threats and the arrest and disarming of Ike Clanton by Virgil Earp. It took less than one minute and only some of the cowboys were armed. When the smoke cleared, Tom and Frank McLowery and Billy Clanton were dead. Virgil and Morgan Earp were seriously wounded and Doc Holliday was grazed by a bullet. Ike Clanton and Billy Claiborne survived the fight by fleeing from the scene. The controversy over the motives and responsibility for the fight began immediately thereafter in the newspapers, in the courts, and in a crescendo of vendettas that saw Virgil Earp wounded, Morgan shot and killed (a half-breed named Indian Charlie was among those charged), and the remaining Earps taking the law into their own hands. These controversies continue even today.

Synopsis of the Plots

My Darling Clementine (1946, 96 minutes, Films, Inc./Key Video)

In 1882 the Earp brothers—Wyatt, Morgan, Virgil, and James—are driving a herd of cattle across Arizona to California. They cross trails with "Old Man" Clanton and his sons, who offer to buy the herd from them. Wyatt refuses and talks to Clanton about going into Tombstone that night for "a shave, maybe...a glass o' beer." Leaving the youngest brother, James (who is engaged), to watch the cattle, the brothers ride into town where Wyatt's shave is interrupted by a drunken Indian shooting up the street. When the town marshal and his deputies refuse to confront Indian Charlie, Wyatt picks up a rock, distracts him, subdues him, and (literally) kicks him out of town. The mayor offers Earp the marshaling job, but Wyatt refuses. When the brothers return to their camp they find James dead and the cattle gone. They return to Tombstone and Wyatt becomes town marshal to track down his brother's killers and so that "maybe when we leave this county, young kids like you will be able to grow up and live safe."

Wyatt settles in and, while playing cards at the Oriental Saloon, encounters the Mexican woman Chihuahua and Doc Holliday. Doc is a former Boston surgeon with civilized manners, a tubercular cough, and a quick and theatrical temper. He owns the saloon and regards Wyatt with suspicion, though in several subsequent scenes he and Wyatt work together to maintain law and order. In one, the Clantons had disrupted a theatrical performance by forcing the actor to go to a Mexican bar to declaim for them. Wyatt and Doc rescue the actor. Though Old Man Clanton apologizes to Earp, when the marshal leaves he horsewhips his sons, telling them "when ya pull a gun, kill a man."

Doc's former fiancée, Clementine Carter, arrives in Tombstone, painfully reminding him of all he has lost. He rudely orders her to "go back home...where you belong," warning that "if you don't, I'm moving on." And to prove that he is no longer the man Clementine remembers, he offers to legitimize his relationship with Chihuahua. Partly out of concern for Doc and partly because of his own growing interest in Clementine, Wyatt tries to intercede with Doc, but this only makes things worse. The next morning, Clementine and Wyatt attend a church dance and the supper that follows. Doc appears and again orders Clementine to leave. After having words with Wyatt, Doc boards a stagecoach and, on its way out of town, throws Chihuahua some money. Understanding that this means good-bye, she rushes upstairs and tries to force Clementine to leave. Wyatt intervenes and in the fracas discovers that Chihuahua is wearing an engraved silver cross that James had bought for his fiancée. Chihuahua claims that Doc gave it to her and Wyatt, infuriated, sets out after Doc. He catches up with him and, against the stark majesty of Monument Valley, shoots Doc's gun from his hand. Together they return to Tombstone to confront Chihuahua.

Chihuahua admits that it was Billy Clanton, not Doc, who gave her the cross. She is shot in the back by Billy, who is spying on her through her window, to silence her.

While Wyatt and Clementine convince Doc to operate on Chihuahua, Virgil chases Billy, mortally wounded in making his escape, back to the Clanton ranch. There he finds that Billy has died and, as he turns to leave the Clantons in their grief, Old Man Clanton shoots Virgil. Despite Doc's efforts to save her, Chihuahua also dies. Old Man Clanton rides into town, dumps Virgil's body on the street, and challenges Wyatt to come for them at the OK Corral.

At dawn the next day Wyatt, joined by Morgan, Doc, and Tombstone's mayor and religious leader (who are left to guard the street) deliberately proceed to the corral and demand that the Clantons "submit to proper authority." Ike Clanton begins shooting and is killed by Wyatt. Doc and Morgan have positioned themselves at the side of the corral. Doc reveals himself by coughing and is shot by Phin and Sam. Morgan then kills Sam, and Doc pulls himself back up and kills Phin, as he himself falls dead, leaving his white handkerchief fluttering from the corral railing. Old Man Clanton then surrenders and Wyatt orders the apparently grief-stricken father to "start wandering." Clanton mounts his horse, but as he rides away, he draws a hidden pistol. Before he can fire, Morgan kills him with three fanned shots. From first shot to last, this rendition of the gunfight takes one minute and forty-five seconds. The film ends with Morgan and Wyatt leaving Tombstone. On the way out of town, they encounter Clementine. Morgan says good-bye and rides on. Clementine tells Wyatt that she is staying in Tombstone to start a school. Wyatt indicates that he may come east again and stop by to see her. The film ends with Wyatt riding off to join his brothers.

Gunfight at the OK Corral (1957, 122 minutes, Films, Inc./ Paramount Home Video)

The film begins with three cowboys riding toward Fort Griffin, Texas, past the boot hill cemetery, to avenge the death of their leader's brother who drew on Doc Holliday. Kate Fisher, who saw the cowboys ride into town, goes to the hotel to warn Doc. She and Doc fight over his "airs" and Doc insists on keeping his "appointment with Mr. Bailey." She represents everything he loathes in himself and he both despises and needs her. While Bailey and his friends wait for Doc in the saloon, U.S. Marshal Wyatt Earp rides into town on the trail of Ike Clanton who "has a dozen counts on him." But the town marshal, Cotton Wilson, has let Clanton slip through his fingers. Shocked by Wilson's apparent abdication of his responsibility, Wyatt goes to the saloon to pick up leads about Ike's plans. He is told that Doc Holliday played cards with Ike. Stopping momentarily to size up Bailey and his friends, Wyatt goes to the hotel to make a deal with Holliday for information. Wyatt tells Holliday that Bailey has a derringer in his boot, but Doc refuses to help him, having been run out of several towns by Earp lawmen. Wyatt returns to the saloon and witnesses the confrontation between Doc and Bailey. Though Holliday kills Bailey in a fair fight, Marshal Wilson arrests him anyway and takes him to the hotel to await a lynch mob. Kate pleads with Earp to help Doc escape this fate and, against his better judgment, he does. Doc and Kate ride past the cemetery on their way out of town as Wyatt watches from his hotel window.

The scene then shifts to a stagecoach coming into Dodge City past its boot hill. (By the way, note that all of these towns look alike and are peopled only by white Anglo-Saxons.) The stage stops and a beautiful woman, Laura Denbo, gets off. Wyatt and Bat Masterson, who has come to borrow Wyatt's deputies to chase down Chief Dull Knife, who is "on a rampage," watch her and ask Wyatt's deputy, Charlie Bassett, who she is. Bassett is more concerned that "Doc Holliday and his lady are in town." Earp lends Masterson all his deputies except Bassett, tells Masterson to have them back before the cattle drives reach town, and then goes off to confront Doc in a barbershop. After some discussion, Wyatt agrees to let Doc stay and gamble on condition that there would be "no knives, no guns, no killing."

That night, Bassett informs Wyatt that Miss Denbo is a professional gambler and that, against Wyatt's ordinance, she is playing in the main room. Aware that women in this position always cause trouble, Wyatt orders her to stop. But a drunken cowboy objects and Wyatt, though himself unarmed, disarms him. He then arrests Miss Denbo for disturbing the peace. Though he offers to release her if she desists from gambling in public, she insists on going to jail. But on a bet, Doc persuades Wyatt to release her on condition that she confine her activities to a side room. Doc and she gamble the night away, while Kate feeds her jealousy with alcohol.

The next day, Wyatt gets word that "Richie Bell and two of his boys held up the bank at Salina, killed the cashier, and are heading this way." With his deputies away, Wyatt agrees to take Doc along, but refuses to deputize him. Together they kill the outlaws and cement their friendship. But when Doc returns, he has a coughing fit. He needs Kate, but she is nowhere to be found. Meanwhile, Wyatt begins courting Laura.

The next day, Doc demands that Charlie tell him where Kate is. Charlie resists and reminds Doc of his promise to Wyatt. But finally he reveals that Kate has taken up residence with Johnny Ringo across the "deadline" in the less respectable part of town. Doc confronts them but, mindful of his promise to Wyatt, refuses to accept Ringo's offer to fight him. Ringo calls him a coward and Doc leaves, as Kate silently expresses her anguish out of his sight.

That evening Wyatt offers to walk Laura home from a church dance and bazaar. While he is off courting her, an old enemy, cattle boss Shanghai Pierce, arrives with his men, including Johnny Ringo, to shoot up the town and teach Earp a lesson. When Charlie Bassett tries to stop them, he is wounded and the drovers invade and break up the dance. But their shooting interferes with Doc's winning streak at blackjack next door, and as Earp confronts Pierce and his men, Doc comes in behind them and takes their guns. When Ringo tries to draw on him, he shoots him in the arm and they are all carted off to jail by the citizenry. Wyatt thanks Doc and calls their debt even, but Doc insists that the tables are still not squared.

The next day Wyatt informs Doc that he and Laura are to be married and that he is quitting his job as a lawman. Doc wishes them well and returns to his hotel room. There Kate is waiting to beg him to take her back, but he says that it is too late for that. She leaves to return to Ringo, swearing that she will see Doc in hell for his rejection of her.

As Wyatt is packing up, Charlie brings him a letter from the attorney general offering him a job as U.S. marshal "whenever you want it" and a telegram from his brother Virgil. He reads it and his whole demeanor changes. On the bluffs outside of town he explains that he must respond to his brother's call for help. But Laura says that she cannot become a lawman's wife, following him from town to town, waiting for the inevitable news that she is a widow. Wyatt rides off, leaving her there.

On Wyatt's way west, Doc Holliday joins him, looking, he says, for healthier climate and a change of luck. The two arrive in Tombstone together, passing its boot hill. Doc checks in at the hotel, while Wyatt proceeds to his brother Virgil's house, where Virgil and Morgan and their families and Jimmie, the youngest brother who is engaged to be married, are awaiting his leadership. After dinner, Virgil lays out the situation. Ike Clanton has organized rustling into a big business and with a corrupt county sheriff (Cotton Wilson) and judge, controls the county. But with the Earps in control of the city, Clanton can't ship his cattle. Virgil is troubled by Doc's presence in Tombstone and Wyatt defends his presence as his responsibility. Wyatt shuts the town to trouble by banning firearms within its limits. He then accepts the marshal's commission, offered earlier, thus superseding the sheriff's power. While Wyatt is waiting for his marshal's commission, he and John Clum's citizen committee turn the Clanton gang away from an Eddie Foy performance at the Schieffelin Theater. At the same time, Kate Fisher arrives in town and is taken to the Clanton ranch by Johnny Ringo, who taunts Doc almost into violating his promise to Wyatt. In stopping him, Virgil advises Doc to get out of Wyatt's life. Doc does in fact decide to leave and bids farewell to Wyatt.

The next day the youngest Clanton, Billy, is arrested for drunkenness. At the same time Wyatt receives his appointment as U.S. marshal. He decides to take Billy home and simultaneously confront Ike with this new situation. The Clantons' mother chides her son and tells Wyatt that "I don't know what I'm going to do with that boy. The way he's going now, he's going to end up like his father, shot down for stealing cattle." Wyatt then talks to the boy about living up to older brothers' reputations and Billy confides to Wyatt that "It's not that I want to be a gunfighter exactly, it's just—I don't know, sometimes I get lonely." Billy then promises to repent. As Wyatt leaves, Ike and Cotton Wilson ride up and make threatening noises, but when Wyatt shows them his marshal's appointment, Ike backs off and again offers him a bribe, which Wyatt rejects. Ike then holds a meeting of his gang and decides to kill Wyatt that evening, forcing the rest of the Earps into a family feud. Kate overhears their plot.

That night Jimmy replaces Wyatt on rounds and is killed in his place. Wyatt finds the body and, despite Doc's warning, vows revenge: a personal fight. For his part, Doc finds Kate and forces her to reveal the names of the killers. He then lunges for her but collapses in a tubercular spasm. Kate flees for her life but is drawn back, believing that Doc is dying. Still later, Billy brings a message from Ike to Wyatt telling him to meet the Clanton gang (Ike, Phin, and Billy Clanton, Frank and Tom McLowery, and Johnny Ringo) at sunup at the OK Corral. Wyatt tells Billy not to join in, but Billy says he must be loyal to his brothers and Wyatt says he understands. Waiting at Virgil's house for sunup, Virgil's wife chastises the Earp brothers for not behaving as lawmen and for rejecting the help of the citizens' committee. Wyatt then goes to Doc's hotel, desperate for his help, but finds him unconscious and watched over by Kate. He returns to his own room filled with despair, staring into the mirror at what he has become.

At dawn, the Clantons ride from their ranch while their mother waits in dread. Doc awakens and, despite Kate's pleas, determines to stand "with the only friend I've ever had." The gang arrives at the OK Corral where they are met by Cotton Wilson, who is sent to try to get Wyatt to meet Ike alone. The Earps and Doc Holliday assemble and begin walking toward the corral. Wilson stops them and delivers his message, but is accused by Doc of being in on Jimmy's killing. Wyatt tells Cotton to get back with his friends. He reports to Ike and asks to be let out. Ike tells him to stand by the horses, but when the gunplay starts, he tries to flee and is shot in the back by Ike. The gunfight begins when Frank McLowery opens fire from his hiding place in a wagon. During its course Morgan is shot by Phin Clanton, who is, in turn, shot by Doc as he rescues Morgan. Wyatt then sets the wagon alight by shooting a kerosene lamp hanging from it and Frank McLowery is set afire. In an attempt to save him, his brother Tom charges Wyatt and is killed by him at close range. Virgil is then shot in the leg by Ike as he attempts to move forward. Wyatt rescues him and when Ike tries to kill the distracted Wyatt, the latter blows him apart with a shotgun blast. Ringo and Billy Clanton try to flank Doc from different sides and Billy grazes Doc in the right arm. Wyatt then wounds Billy in the shoulder but he crawls away. Doc then sees Ringo sneaking behind the horses and, despite his wound, tells Wyatt that "I'll take care of Ringo." Wyatt checks his brothers and sets out after Billy. After some hide-and-seek, Doc kills Ringo with three shots. Grievously wounded, Billy runs down Allen Street to Fly's Photographic Gallery with Wyatt in hot pursuit. Billy breaks in and staggers upstairs to a balcony. Wyatt follows, ordering Billy to give up. Wyatt enters the gallery and Billy wildly shoots at him. Wyatt is unable to fire back, but before Billy can steady his aim, Doc fatally shoots him from outside through the window. Billy tumbles over the balcony and falls dead at Wyatt's feet. Surveying the carnage, Wyatt drops his gun, takes off his badge, and drops it to the ground. The gunfight took exactly seven minutes in this version.

In the gunfight's aftermath, Wyatt comes to the saloon to thank Doc. He says he is going to California to try to find Laura. Doc returns to the gaming table. Wyatt rides past boot hill and off into the frame as the film ends.

Doc (1971, 122 minutes, Films, Inc.)

Out of a dusty windswept desert night, a lone weary rider (Doc Holliday), dressed in black, approaches a run-down Mexican cantina. Inside are a Hispanic bartender, two cowboys playing cards, and a prostitute (Katie Elder). He plays poker with the cowboys (one of whom is Ike Clanton, the other his nephew known only as "the Kid") for the lady's "services." The stranger wins and, after spending the night with her, reluctantly agrees to take her to Tombstone. He tosses some coins on the ground to pay the Mexican for providing them with provisions for the trip, and the Mexican curses them under his breath. Halfway across the desert, they discover that he has filled the canteen with vinegar. They barely make it to the mountains, but, refreshed there, enter Tombstone in style the next morning.

The town is a raucous place, filled with all manner of people—Anglos, Mexicans, Orientals, Indians—of all classes and occupations. Katie Elder is welcomed into a brothel and Doc collapses in his hotel room. The door to his room swings open and a menacing figure enters, rousing Doc. He smiles and embraces his friend Wyatt Earp. The scene shifts to a smoky Alhambra Saloon where the Clantons are drinking. Earp and Doc enter and exchange words. Wyatt then explains the situation in Tombstone. "It's wide open....So you organize the gambling...I'll run the law, we'll both end up rich, very rich." Katie enters and Ike accosts her. Wyatt intercedes and pistol-whips Ike. The cowboys, except for Ike's nephew, the Kid, leave, but Johnny Ringo warns him to watch himself—"that Wyatt Earp ain't right in his head." Holliday interrupts his gambling, asks the Mexican band to play a waltz, and proceeds to dance with Katie, as a concerned Wyatt looks on.

The scene shifts again to Wyatt's house the next day. Virgil and Morgan Earp are wrestling on the ground while Wyatt, his common-law wife Mattie, and Virgil's wife Alie prepare for a political reception. As Wyatt politics for sheriff, off-camera voices explain the relationship between Doc and Wyatt and refer to Doc as Earp's "heavy artillery." Doc is introduced to Wyatt's political opponent, Johnny Behan, and to a skeptical John Clum, editor of the *Tombstone Epitaph*; but as Clum questions him, Doc breaks into a coughing fit and is helped away by Wyatt, who directs him to a "Chinaman" at the end of Allen Street, where he gets high on opium. Upon leaving the opium den, Doc encounters the Kid, who asks him to teach him how to shoot. Doc reluctantly agrees and gives him a lesson the next day, telling him the story of his life in the process.

Back in town Wyatt and Ike again collide. That night Doc has another coughing fit and, concluding that he must do something to change his life, steals Katie from her brothel and sets her up in a small cabin at the edge of town, which she fixes up for the two of them. Domestic bliss ensues, despite the evident disapproval of the arrangement by Wyatt and such "respectable" town dwellers as Alie Earp, who visits Katie in a later scene to advise her to "go to church."

A stagecoach rolls into town with doors flapping and a wounded guard in the box. Wyatt rides to get Doc to join in the search for the holdup men, who stole $80,000 in gold from the stagecoach. After saying good-bye to Katie, they find the empty strongbox on the trail and, guessing that Johnny Ringo is responsible, follow tracks toward the Clanton ranch. At the same time, the Kid informs Ike of the robbery. Ike too concludes that Ringo is the culprit and that he will bring the law down on all of them. Earp and Holliday ride in. Words are exchanged as Ike tells Wyatt that "We don't steal money." Surrounded by Clanton and McLowery men, Ike challenges Earp to a fistfight and beats him severely until Doc stops it. Doc tends his friend's injuries and Wyatt tells him, "I'm gonna kill him." Doc returns with a battered Wyatt to Wyatt's house and, as Doc returns to Katie and domestic bliss, Virgil tells Wyatt that Wells Fargo has offered a $20,000 reward for the stagecoach robbers. Wyatt sends Virgil to set up a meeting with Ike. He plans to offer Ike the reward in return for the bandits. "Ike gets some money," Wyatt says ominously, "we get the credit, then we win the election and we clean up Tombstone," to which Virgil responds, "You mean, clean out Tombstone."

The next day as Wyatt arrests some drunks fighting, Doc and Katie go for a ride in the country. Later, John Clum encounters Doc in the barbershop and asks him why Wyatt wants to be sheriff. Clum suggests that money is the reason and when Doc demurs that Johnny Behan hasn't gotten rich from the job, Clum says that this is because Behan is "dumb and honest." When Doc asks Clum if he thinks that Wyatt is honest, Clum answers, "Nope." Just then, shots ring out across the street. Doc, to his horror, discovers that the Kid has shot a man who drew on him. When Wyatt tries to arrest the Kid, Doc turns on him and Sheriff Behan takes the Kid into custody. Earp looks at his friend in shocked bewilderment.

That night Johnny Behan and Wyatt Earp make speeches at a town rally. Behan talks as a permanent resident of the town and is applauded. Earp responds that he too is in Tombstone to stay, and tells his audience that "there is only one way to get rid of the gun [to insure stability and prosperity] and that is to use the gun....I hope you'll let me get the job done for us, for all our families....I hope you all get home safe." Wyatt and Clum discuss what he (Wyatt) and Doc are after. Clum concludes that while Wyatt wants to win, Doc is searching for something to make his life worthwhile—"some gesture of size."

Later that night the Earps and the Clantons meet on the trail. Earp tells Clanton that he needs Ringo before the election. When Clanton refuses to help Earp win an election that might result in his own death, Wyatt blackmails him by telling him that the Kid is in jail and may be charged with murder if Ike doesn't cooperate. But when Wyatt returns to town, he discovers that Doc has bailed out the Kid. After his release, the Kid tells Holliday that his ambition is "to be just like you" and, in shock, Doc begins to recognize the monster he is creating. When he returns home, Katie asks him for a long-term commitment and Doc recoils in confusion. As Katie reminds him of his mortality, he begins to cough and runs away.

The next morning Virgil informs Wyatt that Doc has bailed out the Kid. Wyatt concludes that the deal is now ruined and that the Clantons must now be killed to silence them. He goes to Doc's house to get him, but Katie doesn't know where he is. Wyatt accuses Katie of changing Doc—of beguiling him sexually. Wyatt finds Doc at the Alhambra, drunk and asleep. Doc greets him with the Spanish phrase "Buenos días, Señor Muerte" (Good morning, Mr. Death). Wyatt tells Doc that there will now be trouble with the Clantons, but Doc responds that Wyatt's trouble is no longer his, that he is sick to death of killing, and that he wants "to leave something behind." Wyatt walks away.

That night, Wyatt plots with his brothers to incite the Clantons into a gunfight. By threatening to bring robbery, conspiracy, murder, and attempted bribery charges against Ike and the Kid, Wyatt plans to force the Clantons to come after him so that he can kill them in self-defense. Virgil and Morgan go off to tell Billy Clanton. A distraught Katie appears and begs Wyatt to help her find Doc. Wyatt suggests that she look for him at "the Chinaman." When she finds him, she berates him and burns the place down. High on opium, Doc tells Katie that they might go away together soon. But Katie, disgusted with him, walks away and Doc turns back to the fire.

The next morning the Clantons and McLowerys ride toward Tombstone. They send the Kid ahead to scout the situation. Wyatt swears in his brothers, now wearing suits, as deputy marshals. The Kid finds Doc at breakfast and explains why the Clantons and McLowerys are coming in. He tells Doc that he will be one of the seven and that he doesn't want to have to kill him. Doc then has his picture taken at Fly's studio, returns to his shack where Katie is packing, and without saying anything, leaves to join the Earps who are arming themselves with pistols and shotguns at the Alhambra. Wyatt and Doc stare at each other, then they walk out onto the street.

The Clantons and McLowerys arrive at the OK Corral where they meet the Kid. Sheriff Behan warns them about gunplay within the town limits, says he doesn't want any trouble, and orders them to give up their guns. Ike refuses and tells Behan to "tell it to the…marshal." Behan then tries to stop the Earps, telling them that the town is his jurisdiction. Earp replies that they can "settle it in court." Clum advises Wyatt that this gunplay will settle nothing, to which Earp responds that "you'd be surprised things you can settle with a gun." And Doc and the three Earps, with shotguns in hand, march towards the corral. Seeing the shotguns, the cowboys spread out. The four enter the corral, and spread out themselves. Ike tells Holliday that this is none of his affair and that they've come to talk. At this point the Earps start firing. Ike and Frank McLowery are hit with the first blast, Billy falls a second later, and a second McLowery is killed by Doc. The Kid draws his pistol and shoots Morgan Earp. Ike tries to get off a shot and Wyatt shoots him with his Buntline special. The Kid and Doc aim at one another, but the Kid relents and holsters his gun, at which point Doc shoots him through his heart. The whole affair takes 20 seconds.

Doc and Wyatt scan the carnage while Virgil announces that Morgan is dead. As a crowd gathers, Doc walks away, half stunned. Wyatt watches him leave and then speaks to the crowd: "They killed my brother; they came to try to destroy everything that we've been trying to build together. But I'm telling you that my brother's death is not going to be in vain, 'cause from this we're going to build a better town—we're going to build a better Tombstone. I swear that to you." The crowd applauds as Virgil looks on incredulously. Doc gets his horse and meets Wyatt on the way out of town. "Why the Kid?" he asks. Doc responds "I guess he reminded me of too many things." The movie ends as he rides away, the street dissolving to the photograph he had taken earlier that day with his name and dates: John H. Holliday, 1852–1887.

For Further Reading

Faulk, Odie B. *Tombstone: Myth and Reality* (Oxford University Press, 1972).

Lyons, Robert, ed. *My Darling Clementine: John Ford Director* (Rutgers University Press, 1984).

Marks, Paula Mitchell. *And Die in the West: The Story of the OK Corral Gunfight* (Simon and Schuster, 1989).

My Darling Clementine (1946, 96 minutes, Films, Inc./Key Video)

Producer: Samuel G. Engel, Twentieth Century-Fox

Director: John Ford

Writers: Samuel G. Engel and Winston Miller from the story by Sam Hellman, based on *Wyatt Earp, Frontier Marshal* by Stuart N. Lake and the reminiscences of Wyatt Earp as told to John Ford

Cinematographer: Joseph P. MacDonald

Cast:

Wyatt Earp .... Henry Fonda

John "Doc" Holliday... Victor Mature

Chihauhua .... Linda Darnell

Clementine Carter .... Cathy Downs

Old Man Clanton .... Walter Brennan

Virgil Earp... Tim Holt

Morgan Earp... Ward Bond

James Earp .... Don Garner

Billy Clanton .... John Ireland

Ike Clanton .... Grant Withers

Sam Clanton .... Micky Simpson

Phin Clanton .... Fred Libby

Granville Thorndike .... Alan Mowbray

Mayor .... Roy Roberts

Kate Nelson... Jane Darwell

Mac the bartender... J. Farrell McDonald

Barber .... Ben Hall

François.. Louis Mercier

Indian troublemaker.. Charles Stevens

Gunfight at the OK Corral (1957, 122 minutes, Films, Inc./Paramount Home Video)

Producer: Hal Wallis, Paramount Pictures

Director: John Sturges

Screenplay: Leon Uris from an article by George Scullin, with sound track including "Gunfight at the OK Corral" sung by Frankie Laine

Cast:

Wyatt Earp .... Burt Lancaster

Doc Holliday... Kirk Douglas

Laura Denbow .... Rhonda Fleming

Kate Fisher .... Jo Van Fleet

Ike Clanton .... Lyle Bettger

Johnny Ringo .... John Ireland

Cotton Wilson... Frank Faylen

Charlie Bassett.. Earl Holliman

Shanghai Pierce.. Ted DeCorsia

Billy Clanton .... Dennis Hopper

John Clum... Whit Bissell

John Shaussey... George Mathews

Virgil Earp.. John Hudson

Morgan Earp... DeForest Kelley

James Earp .... Martin Milner

Bat Masterson .... Kenneth Tobey

Ed Bailey .... Lee Van Cleef

Betty Earp .... Joan Camden

Mrs. Clanton .... Olive Carey

Mayor Kelley .... Nelson Leigh

Tom McLowery... Jack Elam

Drunken cowboy .... Don Castle

Doc (1971, 122 minutes, Films, Inc.)

Producer: Frank Perry, United Artists

Director: Frank Perry

Writer: Peter Hamill

Production designer: Gene Callahan

Cinematographer: Gerald Hirschfield

Cast:

Dr. John Holliday .... Stacy Keach

Wyatt Earp .... Harris Yulin

Katie Elder.. Faye Dunaway

Ike Clanton .... Mike Witney

The Kid .... Denver John Collins

John Clum.. Dan Greenberg

An Earp Filmography:

1. *Law and Order* (1932)

2. *Badmen of Arizona* (1935)

3. *Frontier Marshal* (1939)

4. *My Darling Clementine*(1946)

5. *Gunfight at the OK Corral* (1957)

6. *Cheyenne Autumn* (1964)

7. *Hour of the Gun* (1967)

8. *Doc* (1971)

9. *Sunset* (1988)

Note: Wyatt Earp supposedly appears as an extra in Alan Dwan's *The Half-breed* (1916) starring Douglas Fairbanks. Among the pallbearers at Earp's funeral in 1929 were Western film stars Tom Mix and William S. Hart.

---

* Claims to have used Wyatt Earp as source.

Unit 15: Teaching Media Literacy
Through Film: The OK Corral Gunfight—
A Case Study

Questions Based on the Film

1. What are the characteristics of the West shown in the film? What does it symbolize? Think about the town itself, what its construction materials are, what the interiors look like, and whether certain kinds of things happen in particular

    places in answering the question. _____

    _____

    _____

    _____

2. What kind of people are Wyatt and his brothers? What values do they represent?

    _____

    _____

    _____

3. What kind of people are the Clantons? What motivates their actions?

    _____

    _____

    _____

4. What kinds of people are portrayed in the film? Think about the ethnic and racial composition of the population, the costumes they wear, and whether certain kinds of people play certain kinds of roles in the film as you answer.

    _____

    _____

    _____

5. What kind of person is Doc Holliday in the film? What motivates him?

    _____

    _____

    _____

(continued)

Unit 15: Teaching Media Literacy Through
Film: The OK Corral Gunfight—A Case Study
(continued)

6. What roles do women play in the film? What does the film tell you about a
    woman's place? _____

    _____

    _____

7. In the film, Doc is torn between the values of his past life in the East and his
    current situation. How is this struggle portrayed in the film? _____

    _____

    _____

8. How is the relationship between Wyatt and Doc explained in the film? How is
    their cooperation and friendship justified? _____

    _____

    _____

9. What causes the gunfight to happen in the film? What motivates the two sides to
    confront one another in this way? _____

    _____

    _____

10. Who is right and who is wrong in the film? Why? _____

    _____

    _____

Name _____   Date _____

Unit 15: Teaching Media Literacy Through Film: The OK Corral Gunfight—A Case Study

Comparison Sheet

1. How do the films' portrayals of the West in the early 1880's differ from one another? How might you explain these differences? _____

   _____

   _____

2. How does the portrayal of the Earps change? What does this tell you about how our perceptions of ourselves and our heroes have changed over these decades?

   _____

   _____

   _____

3. How do the portrayals of the Clantons and their motivations change? What does this tell you about the country's images of villainy at the times these films were made? _____

   _____

4. What differences exist in the portrayals of the people and their roles in the films? What does this say about our consciousness of and sensitivity to racial and ethnic diversity and stereotypes when each of these films was made? _____

   _____

   _____

5. How do Doc's personality and motives change in the films? When Doc is compared to the Clantons, what can be learned about perceptions of good and evil in the world at the time each film was made? _____

   _____

   _____

(continued)

Name _____   Date _____

Unit 15: Teaching Media Literacy Through Film:
The OK Corral Gunfight—A Case Study *(continued)*

6. By comparing women's roles in the films, what changes occurred with respect to the filmmakers' perceptions of "a woman's place" over these decades? _____

_____

_____

7. How does Doc's inner struggle change in the different films? What does his treatment of the women in his life tell us about a man's psyche at the times these films were made? _____

_____

_____

8. How does the Wyatt–Doc relationship change among films? Does this justification help us to understand such things as America's cooperation with Stalin against Hitler in World War II, or the country's willingness to put up with dictators in the struggle against communism during the cold war?

_____

_____

9. How do notions of personal greed, community, duty, and family loyalty as motivating factors change in the films? How are these valued as the Earps and the Clantons collide in each film? _____

_____

_____

10. How do our ideas of heroism and villainy change among the films? What does this tell us about the time in which each film was made? _____

_____

_____

11. Which of the films most accurately tells the story of the gunfight at the OK Corral? Why? _____

_____

_____

© 1994 J. Weston Walch, Publisher   120   *American History on the Screen*

About the Authors

Wendy S. Wilson has been a teacher in the Lexington, Massachusetts, Public Schools since 1971. She has taught social studies in grades 7–12, was appointed interim social studies department head, and served as the cable television specialist systemwide. She also is a senior lecturer in history at University College, Northeastern University, and team teaches a graduate course in history and media with Gerald Herman. She has been a frequent presenter at conferences such as the International Conference on Technology and Education, the National School Board Association's Conference on Technology, the New England Museum Educators, and the Historian's Film Committee of the American Historical Association. She was the only public school teacher asked to serve on a task force titled "The Historian and Moving-Image Media," which was funded by the National Endowment for the Humanities and the American Historical Association. As a program developer and on-camera presenter, she has hosted two series on the Columbus Quincentennial shown on the Mass LearnPike, the educational satellite network of the Massachusetts Corporation for Educational Telecommunications.

Gerald H. Herman is a tenured assistant professor of history and special assistant to the office of the general counsel at Northeastern University. He is the author of a nine-part multimedia presentation and anthology on the culture of World War I entitled *World War I: The Destroying Fathers Confirmed* and of an award-winning National Public Radio program called "War" on the same subject. He also has written extensively on history and film including analyses of individual films, teacher guides for both secondary schools (*World History on the Screen*) and colleges, bibliographical references (including the media section of *The Craft of Public History* published by Greenwood in 1983) and currently serves as media editor for *The Public Historian*. As a media writer and producer he created a forty-program, instructional television history of Western civilization, "Windows on the Past," and a video for the National Council on Public History, "Public History Today." He has just completed work on a radio exploration of the culture of World War II entitled "The Sound in the Fury" for National Public Radio and is writing a comprehensive *Historians' Guide to Films*.